Fireworks and Folly

Fireworks and Folly

How We Killed Minnie Sutherland

by
John Nihmey

Philip
Diamond
Books
Inc.

First published 1998.

Canadian Cataloguing in Publication Data

Nihmey, John
Fireworks and Folly

ISBN 0-921043-05-8

1. Sutherland, Minnie.
2. Indians, Treatment of — Canada.
3. Indian women — Canada — Biography.
I. Title.

E90.S83N541998 971'.00497'0092 C98-900434-1

Designed by Fortunato Aglialoro
Falcom Design & Communications, Inc.

Jacket photograph by Paul von Baich
Photograph of Hull strip by Michel Lafleur, © *Le Droit*, Ottawa, Centre for Research on French Canadian Culture, Fonds Le Droits, C71, Ph92/220289/5-5A

Philip Diamond Books Inc.
500-1145 Hunt Club Road, Ottawa, Canada K1V 0Y3

Distributed by Hushion House Publishing Limited

Printed in Canada

NOTES AND ACKNOWLEDGEMENTS

This book is a work of non-fiction narrative. Interspersed throughout the narrative are media clips, police statements, court testimony, interview quotations, and excerpts from official documents. In the narrative I have tried my best to accurately depict real events. Where it was necessary to present a character's thoughts or words, I have taken great care to avoid putting words in people's mouths or thoughts in their heads. In instances of hearsay I have used quotations to highlight spoken words; in cases where personal instinct provided the thought, I have used italics. To deal with cases of conflicting testimony, I have departed from the narrative and included the testimony of all witnesses involved, in order to let readers draw their own conclusions. In one instance, where witnesses to the same event had unique renditions, yet the truth appeared obvious to me, I have described the event in the narrative and also included the conflicting testimony.

In a work of this nature, the true testimony to its existence is the input of the people who lived the story being told. To all the people who took the time to speak with me and my researcher, even when the discussion proved painful, I would like to express my deepest gratitude. Special thanks is extended to Roseanne Sutherland, David Nahwegahbow, Patrick Smith, David Knox, Michel Filion, Maggie Bugden, Evelyn Mark, Linda and John Wynne, Joyce Wesley, Christy and David Wesley, and Doreen and Tim Milbury. Thanks also to Carole St-Denis; Lorraine DeGrace; Cecil (Tom) Thomas; Dave Ethier of J. R. Dallas; unnamed staff and management of Le Boule (previously Mexi-Go); Willy Eyamie of the Castel restaurant; Barb Conlin, Sherry Halgerson, Sandra Barnaby and Heather Black of the Dalhousie Health and Community Services Centre; Kashechewan chiefs

Jonathan Solomon and Andrew Reuben; Kashechewan elders Dorothy Friday and Willy Wesley, Jr.; Dr. Gwynne Jones and Dr. Margaret Peacock of the Ottawa General Hospital; Marie Louise Boudreau and Carl Hudon of the Sisters of Charity Detoxification Centre; Vince Kicknosway and Jim Eagle of the Odawa Native Friendship Centre; 18 Lowrey Street landlady Rosalie MacMillan; 18 Lowrey Street tenant Michael Bellefeuille; Reverend James Froh of the Native People's Parish in Toronto; Karen Irving of The Well; Fran McGovern; Madeleine Blundon; Madeline Kiokee; Sidney Goodwin, Daisy Arthur; Hannah Wesley; Joseph Renaud; Kelly Madore; Maurice Prud'homme of the Racine, Robert and Gauthier funeral home; Sergeant Luc Givogue of the Ottawa Police Department; Steve Bindman of Southam News; and John S. Long.

Many people provided encouragement, guidance, and help in the evolution of this book: Jennifer Swanson David, my prime researcher, assumed the difficult task of trying to locate many of the people listed above, finding and eventually interviewing even the most physically isolated and emotionally remote people. Jennifer Glossop, my editor, helped to keep me focused on my purpose for writing the book, continually making sure that the stops on my literary journey did not become more important that the journey itself. My advisers, Morty Mint and Alison Maclean, provided encouragement from the start, tempering arguments on the book's marketability with confidence in the book-buying public. The staff at NIVA Inc. and Philip Diamond Books provided invaluable creative assistance: in particular, Ann Fothergill-Brown and Dalya Goldberger, who provided editorial input and encouragement throughout the project. Finally I would like to remember my dog, Robinson, who demanded nothing during the six years I spent researching and writing this book, and who fell asleep forever the night I wrote the last page.

To Linda Wynne

—Within society,
there are always those who care.

The day the story broke, the three editions of the *Ottawa Citizen* each told its own version of the episode. Though culled from the same reporter's notes, each story brandished a different headline and focus. It was as if the reporter had decided from the start that the events alone would be insufficient to generate enough outrage.

The woman at the centre of this macabre whodunit was portrayed a stoic. A Cree Indian, Minnie Sutherland was of simple means, legally blind but active. Her job at a community health centre helped support two daughters living up north. Diabetic and forbidden to drink alcohol, she had set out with thousands of others on New Year's Eve to watch the fireworks on Parliament Hill. Although her destination was known, it was not clear how she ended up across the river in Hull, Quebec, unconscious in a snowbank.

The crime seemed so obvious that I slept easily that night. Without a doubt, this was a clear case of police officers stereotyping a native woman as a drunk; bad cops who would pay the price for their cruel and insensitive actions.

But in the days that followed, updated reports made the circumstances surrounding Minnie's death more convoluted.

THE OTTAWA CITIZEN, JANUARY 14, 1989

Key witnesses in death appear

Hearing about Minnie's death in the media, a woman named Carole St-Denis notified the Hull police that it was her car that had come into contact with Minnie. Now that St-Denis had surfaced, the driver's "disappearance" was less of a mystery, and her explanation for leaving the scene of an accident quite plausible: the police had asked her to leave. Minnie had walked into her car while trying to cross the street and had fallen. In an effort to keep the traffic moving, the officers had insisted that St-Denis move her car, assuring her that everything was under control. Were the officers aware that Minnie had been in an accident? Hull police sergeant Yves Martel didn't think so, stating that the officers might have thought Minnie had been drinking. As for leaving her alone in a snowbank, apparently the officers assumed that the woman who was with her would take care of her.

THE OTTAWA CITIZEN, JANUARY 15, 1989

Police told woman was in mishap: cousin

As soon as Minnie's companion that evening, her cousin, Joyce Wesley, had a chance to tell her side of the story, the police force from Ottawa, the Ontario city across the river from Hull, became entangled in the controversy. Joyce said that after getting Minnie off the snowbank in Hull, three university students helped bring her to a nearby restaurant. There, Minnie became ill. A stranger offered to drive Joyce and Minnie back to Ottawa. But nobody, not even Joyce, knew where Minnie lived. After realizing that they were driving around the wrong area of town, Joyce and the driver noticed that Minnie had lost consciousness. They stopped the car and laid her on the sidewalk while they called 911. But the ambulance that arrived on the scene left empty moments later, and the police officer who loaded Minnie into the back of her cruiser didn't ask for Joyce's name or phone number, even after supposedly being told that Minnie had been hit by a car.

THE OTTAWA CITIZEN, JANUARY 16, 1989

Police deny being told of accident

The Hull police, after receiving a scathing letter from Dr. Gwynne Jones of the Ottawa General Hospital, went on the defensive and denied any knowledge of Minnie Sutherland being involved in a car accident. Dr. Jones's letter described how, for three days after her admission to hospital, the cause of Minnie's injuries were unknown. Until, that is, a university student who had witnessed the accident called in. Dr. Jones went on to say that, owing to the lack of this crucial information, the hospital had wasted precious time with unnecessary treatment. Rumours started about a public inquiry, but one was unlikely: something about different laws in Ontario and Quebec that might make it difficult for an inquest on one side of the river to subpoena witnesses from the other.

THE OTTAWA CITIZEN, JANUARY 19, 1989

Coroner calls inquest into woman's death

I was amazed at the breakneck speed with which the Ontario government acted. I knew that the Hull Police Department had already started its own internal investigation, and learned that the Ottawa Police Department was going to start its own, too. But public inquiries aren't that easily put together, particularly because they involve taxpayer money. Public interest aside, the Native Women's Association of Canada had spoken up, saying that the entire case smacked of racial overtones. Next, the powerful Assembly of First Nations became involved, giving the incident a sense of national importance that was bound to result in some form of official response.

༆

The inquest was to be held at the provincial courthouse in downtown Ottawa, a kilometre west of where Joyce and her escorts had rested Minnie on the sidewalk while they called 911 from a pay phone. A date had yet to be set, but under direct order from Ontario provincial coroner Dr. Ross Bennett, the local coroner for Ottawa would not supervise. Instead, because of the enormous public interest in the case, as well as the potentially serious political overtones, the inquest would be presided over by Dr. Walter Harris, regional coroner for Eastern Ontario.

Later that month, attention once again focused across the river as an internal Hull Police Department report declared that racism played no part in the treatment of Minnie Sutherland. The report further stated that Joyce Wesley had assured police she would take care of her cousin after she had *fallen*. Joyce publicly denied having said this and accused the police of a cover-up. Meanwhile, a statement by François Hamon, head of Hull's bar association, did little to dispel Joyce's allegations: "It wasn't a good judgement call that Hull police investigated themselves," he said, revealing that the city's lawyers would likely approve a resolution asking the Quebec Police Commission to conduct an independent inquiry into the matter.

$\mathcal{S}$

The Coroner's Inquest into the Death of Minnie Sutherland began on Wednesday, February 22, 1989.

Minnie Sutherland's nineteen-year-old daughter, Roseanne, flew down from Timmins, Ontario, accompanied by her aunt, Linda Wynne, and Linda's husband, John. It was Roseanne's second trip to Ottawa this winter; she had come just weeks earlier to pick up her deceased mother's personal belongings. Both times, her nine-year-old sister, Violet, remained with her cousins at the family home in Kashechewan, in Northern Ontario.

David Nahwegahbow, a young native lawyer new in practice and determined to crusade for justice toward his people, was hired to represent Roseanne at the inquest and in any other legal matters pertaining to Minnie's death. The incidents surrounding Minnie's death smacked of all the issues that had convinced Nahwegahbow to become a lawyer; by the time the local native Friendship Centre had contacted him about taking the case, he was already on board.

Nahwegahbow was given immediate standing at the inquest; as the representative for Minnie's family, he easily met the criteria of being "substantially and directly interested in the inquest." Robert Côté, who represented the City of Hull, was also given standing. He made it clear that the testimony of the two Hull police officers he represented were outside the court's jurisdiction, but that the men were prepared to co-operate. Lawyer Sharon McIvor requested standing on behalf of the Native Women's Association of Canada but was denied; she ended up joining Nahwegahbow as co-counsel. An attorney representing Minnie's cousin, Joyce Wesley, was also present, but not to request standing—he just wanted to identify himself with respect to his client.

Outside Courtroom 30 tension mounted. All of the people who had encountered Minnie on New Year's Eve and in the early hours of the following morning had either been subpoenaed or, if they were a Quebec resident, asked to attend. Television, radio, and print media mingled with the witnesses they had previously interviewed; other witnesses kept their distance from the crowd for fear of saying something that would compromise their later testimony. When the doors finally opened, the room filled quickly, leaving few seats for the flock of citizens who had appeared at the inquest hoping to attend.

In his opening remarks, the coroner explained to the jury the function of an inquest. Unlike a criminal trial, he said, which seeks to lay blame or determine guilt, a coroner's inquest is held to "ascertain facts, focus attention on preventible deaths, and satisfy the community that the circumstances surrounding the death of any of its members will not be overlooked, concealed, or ignored."

Roseanne sat next to her aunt Linda in the second row. Her purposeful gaze was in sharp contrast to Linda's look of reserve. Linda did not want her sister's life laid out before a roomful of strangers, especially those whom she felt had contributed to her death. Roseanne, on the other hand, was determined to discover the truth, and remained hopeful that, at least in death, her mother would be served justice.

The coroner introduced Andrejs Berzins, the Crown Attorney and, technically, the coroner's counsel for the proceedings. Berzins picked up where the coroner left off and repeated how the recommendations made by the jury would be critical in preventing future deaths of this nature. He then presented the witnesses that would be called, starting with two character witnesses who could tell the jury what Minnie Sutherland had been like as a friend and a relative.

One by one, the other witnesses were summoned; each one would be examined and cross-examined about their actions the night of Minnie Sutherland's death and in the days that followed. Among them was Joyce Wesley, who was called upon to justify her allegations of a police cover-up and to describe a New Year's Eve celebration gone sour. Her uncertainty about what happened that night set the tone for the entire inquest.

Coroner's Inquest Testimony – Joyce Wesley

Q. Her name, Minnie, was that a nickname or was that her full name?

A. It was her full name.

Q. O.K. She was also quite small in size, though, right?

A. Yes.

Q. How would you describe her size?

A. She was small, and I was bigger than her.

Q. O.K. And we know from some of the medical records that she was just under five feet, and that's quite small. Was she that small?

A. Yes.

Q. O.K. And just 110 pounds or 115 pounds, I think we...

A. Yes.

Q. All right. She wore glasses?

A. Yes.

Q. What was the situation as far as her eyesight is concerned? How did that affect her?

A. Well, she could see with her glasses on.

Q. Um-hmm.

A. But I don't know–I don't know if she could see without them, I don't know.

Part One

THE SUN

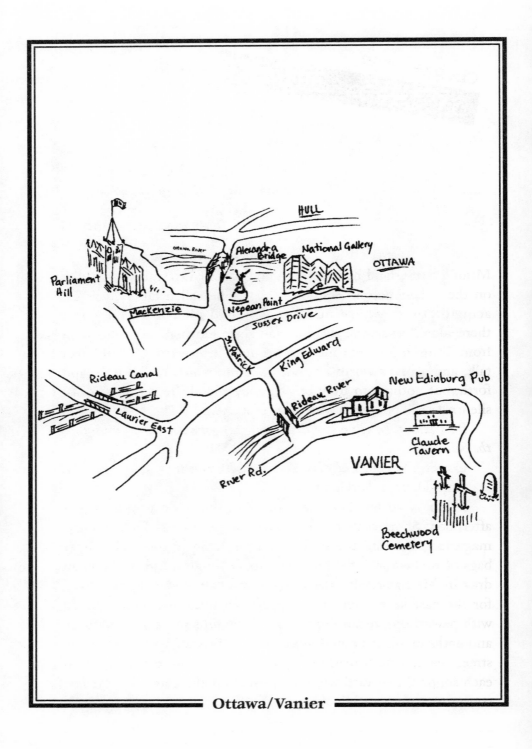

Ottawa/Vanier

Chapter One

When I spoke to her, she said she was going to stay in. She didn't have any money to go out.

— ROSEANNE SUTHERLAND

Minnie Sutherland had spent a good part of December 31, 1988, on the telephone, restless and fidgety. She called family, friends, acquaintances whose numbers she had picked up here and there–almost everyone she had met since moving back to Ottawa from Toronto fourteen months before. There was plenty of small talk, and a year's worth of understanding words tossed back and forth, but nothing to truly brighten her mood. Between the calls, silence, as she pondered who next to phone.

Best friend Maggie Bugden? *No, she's gone back to Chisasibi for the holidays.*

Cousin Doreen? *I already spoke with her two times.*

Aunt Daisy in Kirkland Lake? *She'll cheer me up.*

Minnie had left her one-room dwelling a dozen times that afternoon. Short visits to the corner variety store to look through magazines. Around the back of the building to toss half-empty bags of rubbish into the bin. Over to Wellington Street, the main drag in Mechanicsville, the Ottawa borough where she had lived for the past year. Even that trip offered little distraction. Lined with pawnshops, repair depots, used furniture and clothing stores, and undistinguished diners whose heyday was forty years gone, the street was not particularly inviting. Especially so in winter, when each shop's thin-paned windows frosted up and concealed the few consumer items worth looking at.

Like many who lived in Mechanicsville, Minnie had come to regard the place she called home as little more than a refuge for those who couldn't afford a better place. Over the past few months she had accepted that Mechanicsville was a place where, short of emergencies, like water pouring into a basement or gasoline leaking into the ground, nothing ever got fixed. She had also learned, through experience, that for every frustrated or angry resident in the neighbourhood, a potential tenant on the city's roll was ready to move in.

On this day, the uneven roads that zigzagged through the twenty-odd blocks of Mechanicsville looked more inhospitable than ever. The smattering of Christmas lights that framed windows and decorated trees did little to divert Minnie's attention from the kicked-in garbage cans out front, the motorbikes leaking oil into the snow, and the dented cars parked right up to the watermarked foundations of the houses.

A sombre state of mind made it difficult for her to imagine beyond the season. Instead, she remembered asphalt where lawns and gardens belonged, cracked sidewalks under the ice, one too many vehicles in front of each shingled dwelling—characteristics she had barely noticed last summer.

She hadn't always felt this way; only months earlier she was selling the merits of Mechanicsville to just about anyone who would listen.

Shortly after Minnie had moved in, her landlady at 18 Lowrey Street, Mrs. MacMillan, had told her about the area's historical significance as a working-class village that had become popular early in the century when factories lined the Ottawa River's shores on its northern edge.

Always ready to glean a romantic end from every story told to her, Minnie had likened Mechanicsville to any other community torn apart by hardship but determined to return to prosperity. One day, she had thought, the houses will return to single residences, cobblestone lanes will replace the narrow roads now full of potholes and bumps, and pastry shops will open where junky groceterias now stood. She had even voiced hope for Wellington Street, saying that once the city kicked out the crooked proprietors making money off of everyone's misery, they could restore the buildings and open shops with the kinds of clothes, jewellery, and knick-knacks that even tourists would flock to buy.

During the time that Minnie was enthusiastic about Mechanicsville—her first six months there—she was equally optimistic about finding a job. When she had first returned to Ottawa from Toronto in the fall of 1987, she immediately registered for social welfare—a common practice among native people to alleviate worries while trying to get settled in the city. After a few weeks, she started a job search, knowing from the start it wouldn't be easy. But not for the reasons she believed. Most of Minnie's friends and acquaintances—the native ones, anyway—were perplexed by Minnie's refusal to believe that being, and looking, native had anything to do with her difficulty in finding a job. But Minnie's conviction, even combined with an open and friendly personality, only helped to coax a smile from someone across an employment centre counter; it rarely landed her a job referral. Yet time after time she would insist, "It's my lack of qualifications."

Coroner's Inquest—Cross Examination – Maggie Bugden

Q. But was there any mistaking the fact that she was a native person? To anybody seeing her on the street?

A. Oh no.

Q. She was clearly...

A. She was a native person.

Q. Her appearance.

A. Yes, her appearance was native.

Her visual impairment had been another, equally noticeable, roadblock. The thick bifocals that enabled her to distinguish more than shapes and colours riveted everyone's attention the moment she entered a room. For those who knew her, the glasses were part of Minnie's look, much like her petite form, her dazzling dresses, and her scurrying little legs. But for potential employers, it was hard to see past the thick lenses through which she stared wide-eyed.

Minnie had remained optimistic though, clipping opportunities from the newspaper's Want Ads and asking virtually everyone she met if they knew of any jobs–*anything*–that she could do.

Minnie prepared supper for herself earlier than usual that evening, just after five o'clock. She had come to terms with the prospect of staying in this New Year's Eve, alone, and was anxious to get each of the evening's chores over with. She was also determined to suffer through the next day by herself as well, despite an invitation from her cousin, Doreen Milbury, to spend the day with her, her husband, Tim, and the kids. After supper, she felt proud of herself for remembering that feeling lonely was not the same as feeling desperate.

Minnie had good reason to want to excuse herself from the festivities; 1988 had by no means been a joyous year for her. No sooner had she landed a job at the Dalhousie Health and Community Services Centre when the position came to an end. Then news arrived that her father was losing his battle with colon cancer; the disease had spread to his lungs.

The news devastated Minnie. Bart Sutherland was the one person Minnie truly respected; his was the character upon which Minnie modelled her own. Bart was a man of conviction, determined to assume life's responsibilities, like holding down a job and supporting a family, but not willing to do so at the expense of his spirit. His ability to sit on the band council and carve social policy one moment, and sit by the river whittling with the other men the next, demonstrated his calm acceptance of the world in which he lived. It was also an ideal to which Minnie continually aspired.

Minnie's mother, Margaret—Maggie to everyone who knew her—had little in common with Minnie except a degree of stubbornness that kept both women firmly entrenched in their views about everything. That, and a long list of physical ailments, including diabetes, which had already left Maggie blind for the past decade and which was well on its way to having the same devastating effect on Minnie.

Years earlier, when the family was all together, Maggie was forever seeking to exercise some control over her two daughters, Minnie and Linda, and to caution them against making the mistakes others had made. One of nine children born in the bush near a trap line on the Albany River, Maggie had lived in northern communities all her life. Poised and physically beautiful, Maggie made every effort to satisfy the traditional expectations of her parents, Barbara and Thomas Goodwin. And one of those expectations was to remain dignified and pure.

While she faltered from time to time, Maggie Goodwin was as close to a model child as anyone in her circle, and became a wife and mother of equal repute. A first-hand witness to the evolution of her people and the uneasy blending of native and whites in mixed communities, she knew that having children at a young age and out of wedlock had become increasingly common. The situation left Maggie and other matriarchs in her Cree community with a constant fear of what effect the enticements of sex and alcohol would have on their children. She urged Minnie and Linda to be wary of men who make promises of forever in order to coax young girls into sleeping with them. "Nine months later," Maggie would say, "you're sixteen with a lifelong responsibility before you've even decided if you want to finish school." As she gave these warnings, she would hold her firstborn, Sidney, close, a hint to Minnie and Linda that their mother was talking from experience.

Despite the words of caution, Minnie was determined to forge her life on her own terms, and in places of her choice. She made no bones about being bored with life in Moose Factory, and spoke passionately about towns and cities she knew little about. With men she was awkward and insecure, telling a good joke rather than acting flirtatious. But Minnie was clearly interested in some form of belonging other than to her family. At first, her mother tried subtle persuasion, hoping that her own triumph over the past would alter the course she so feared. But Minnie perceived her mother's advice as an attempt at control, and as a ploy to coax Minnie into doing something practical like getting married and settling down. By the time Minnie was eighteen and ready to leave for school in Ottawa, the two women were spending more time avoiding issues than dealing with them.

More spiritual than any of her children, Maggie combined her Christian upbringing with Cree traditions and a reverence for premonitions. Her belief that a spirit could enter your life through dreams and accompany you through life's trials gave her great comfort.

Despite her deference to spirits, Maggie was, like Minnie, a pragmatist who was not about to leave her or her family's future in the hands of any spirit but her own. Maggie's search for meaning in her life took place in the native community into which fate had guided her; Minnie's was staged on the streets of the various cities to which she was drawn. And in much the same way that Minnie's demeanour brought smiles and salutations from strangers, Maggie's drove fear into friends and acquaintances alike. Indeed, no one on duty at the grocery store in Kashechewan relished the idea of telling Maggie that they were out of a particular cooking staple she needed.

❧

Although Minnie had called almost all her friends and relatives that day—some of them two and three times—she had yet to call

Kashechewan, finding herself alternating between wishing she could delay making the call home as long as possible and wanting to get it over with right away. She decided while eating supper that the best way to handle her dilemma was to coax herself into a better state of mind, in case she sounded depressed over the phone and elicited a similar response from her family members, especially her youngest daughter, Violet, who would already be lonely spending the holidays without her.

She tried to muster some enthusiasm by rummaging through the keepsakes she carried with her from one city to the next: the envelope of photos that showed her with some of her favourite boyfriends; the embroidered tea towels with the satin trim; the lavender sachets tucked in among her clothes. When that didn't work, she set her sights on rearranging the contents of her dresser drawers. At one point, she accidentally caught her profile in the big mirror outside the bathroom door. For the rest of the evening she avoided looking in any other mirrors, remembering a time when posing in front of the glass was part of her weekly ritual before heading out for a night on the town.

✂❧

Her eldest daughter, Roseanne, called from Timmins sometime before seven o'clock, just as Minnie was watching the end of the six o'clock news on CJOH.

Roseanne's soothing voice was the perfect antidote.

"The holidays will be over before you know it," Roseanne told her. Her matter-of-fact advice always had a way of putting Minnie's worries into perspective.

They spoke for a half hour; Roseanne did most of the talking, telling Minnie about her baby son, about how she had survived Christmas in North Bay with her husband's family, and about how her aunt Linda had made sure that Violet enjoyed Christmas despite Grandpa being dead and both mother and sister being absent. In the end, she explained, Minnie probably hadn't missed anything, because even the cookies Linda made at Christmas were likely washed down with a lot of depressing talk from her grandmother. She lamented about how quick the holidays were passing and how she would be back at school in a couple of days.

Speaking with Roseanne gave Minnie the courage to call the family in Kashechewan. One of Linda's children answered the phone cheerfully, instantly challenging Minnie to sound equally happy. When she didn't, the child passed the phone to Linda, who sounded surprised to hear that Minnie had no plans for New Year's Eve. *Not Minnie.* Linda gave her big sister a quick rundown on what they were doing that evening, updated her with news on their brother, Sidney, who still popped in for a visit every day, and quietly confided in her what she and her husband, John, had been dealing with since their father had died. After assurances were given that Violet had managed to have a nice Christmas despite Minnie's absence, Linda passed the phone to her mother.

As expected, Maggie was cranky and instantly began chastising Minnie for not being with the family for the holidays. As usual, this line of conversation resulted in a discussion about Maggie's medical problems, which included gangrene in one leg, and about how she was refusing to have another operation. *Tell me about it*, thought Minnie, who in recent years had endured her own share of operations, including five on her eyes and one for an overactive thyroid that had made her neck swell to twice its size.

She spoke last to Violet, a short but gratifying dialogue about the daily experiences of the nine-year-old. Violet accepted, but did not understand, Minnie's long absence. She knew that her mother cared for her deeply and wanted to hear every detail about what she was doing. Violet asked when Minnie was coming back, and was silently accepting when her mother said, "Well, if I could get a job I would bring you here to live with me tomorrow." The words that brought her daughter pleasure saddened Minnie; she knew that there was no chance of acting on any whim—let alone ambition—where Violet was concerned. Not with Maggie discouraging her from even sending Violet birthday or Christmas presents. At the end of the conversation, Minnie hoped that one day Violet would understand.

ça

By nine o'clock Minnie was in her nightclothes, resigned to spending the rest of the evening watching Dick Clark's "Rockin' New Year's Eve." Before the show started, she dialled the number of someone she had been trying to reach all day: Evelyn Mark, the first native person she met after her first move to Ottawa more than twenty years ago.

"Evelyn, thank God you're there. I thought I'd go bugs today."

Chapter Two
MY MOTHER'S MOCCASINS, ANYONE?

*We used to go out a lot. Minnie would
be sitting there and the next thing you
know there would be men around us.
She loved to mingle.*

— EVELYN MARK

Evelyn listened to Minnie recount the "highlights" of her day and agreed that they didn't amount to much, then admitted that she didn't have any plans either.

"At least you live in Vanier," Minnie said, recalling a time when even the simplest activities, like strolling down old Montreal Road or sharing fries from a chipwagon with a friend, brought her instant enjoyment. "There's always something going on there."

This was not the first time that Evelyn had heard Minnie reminisce over the "good old days" in Vanier, the earthy, French-speaking community east of Ottawa that had welcomed both women to the nation's capital twenty-two years before. And while she had only lived there for little more than a year over two decades ago, Minnie still spoke of Vanier as if it were home.

৪৯

Minnie and Evelyn first met in Ottawa in 1966. The two women, together with Maggie Bugden, a young Cree woman whom Minnie had befriended around the same time, attended adult education classes offered by the local board of education. For a time, the three women boarded at the same house in Vanier.

Living in Vanier and going to school in Ottawa gave Minnie a feeling of independence that she would never have experienced had she ceded to her mother's wishes and stayed with the family up north. Here, she derived great joy from the simplest activities, like dressing up in something colourful and window-shopping, or telling their landlady the news about school. Unlike the average day in Moose Factory, where she spent half her time dreaming of being elsewhere, in Vanier, Minnie was content to think about how great it was to be there.

❧

Just before Christmas 1966, Minnie left to visit her family up north and didn't return. While she, Evelyn, and Maggie Bugden continued to correspond by mail, it was more than twenty years before Minnie would return to Ottawa, this time destitute and unhappy, on Halloween 1987.

Evelyn took Minnie in, aware that her old friend had developed a sporadic drinking problem and had endured numerous operations that had failed to save her eyesight from deteriorating to near blindness. Together with Maggie Bugden, and with the help of Minnie's cousins Doreen and Tim Milbury, she set out to resurrect the once-vivacious Minnie and make up for lost time.

Coroner's Inquest Testimony – Tim Milbury

Q. All right. As far as using alcohol or drinking, were you aware of any problem that she had?

A. No, Minnie didn't–to me, Minnie didn't have a problem with alcohol. I don't even know what kind of drinker she was, if she was a drinker.

Minnie learned about the one-room apartment in Mechanicsville after she had been staying with Evelyn for only a few days. The morning after her reunion with Evelyn and Maggie, she frequented the Odawa Native Friendship Centre for food stamps and information on where to find cheap clothing and accommodation. As it turned out, the centre had just received notice that a furnished flat in Mechanicsville was available. Sight unseen, Minnie took it.

Vince Kicknosway, from the Friendship Centre, drove Minnie to the apartment the day she moved in. During the ride over, she couldn't contain her enthusiasm, and prattled on about how close she would be to downtown. Before Vince was even out of the car, Minnie had collected her two boxes of belongings and was racing up the eight steps that led to the first-floor walk-in at 18 Lowrey. At the door, she invited Vince in for some tea and cookies, and became excited when he accepted. While boiling water in the blackened kettle she found beneath the sink, she mumbled about how she would have to get the place fixed up, and asked where she might get a used television. Vince just smiled, thinking how much better the place would look after a few weeks under Minnie's care. He wondered, though, how long her optimism would last without a job.

Once settled, Minnie made a point of getting organized, and letting all her friends and relatives know that she had moved to Ottawa and, yes, she was living in her own apartment—not a rooming house, not a friend or cousin's house, and not on the street. One of the first relatives she got in touch with was her mother's sister, Daisy Arthur, who lived in Kirkland Lake.

Like Minnie, Daisy had never met Maggie Sutherland's expectations, and would easily appreciate Minnie's news of landing, amidst obstacles, on her feet once again.

Letter to Daisy Arthur – Minnie Sutherland

Dear Daisy,

How are you these days? As for myself I'm not to bad at

all. I have moved to Ottawa last month now. It's nice but

very quiet for me. At least I have my friends here, so once in
a while we go to the Bingos.

I haven't been looking for any job or reapplying for school
yet. But I should be able too sometimes after the New year.
It didn't take me long to find an apartment, I thought I would
had a hard time. I stayed with my girlfriends at her place for
four days. After that I went for apartment hunting. I just
found it same day, I also had my phone put in. So if you
want to phone me up the no. is 613-728-8070. Now I just
need some furniture and some other items, dressers. So what I
did was I put a wanted ad in the penny saver paper for just
donations only. And I'll be getting some calls from people
now. Guess what Daisy while I was writing this letter the telephone rang. This guy asked me am I the person who needs the
furniture. He said he had a couch that was in a good cond-
tion also an arm chair. He started asking me questions about
me, where I came from all that jazz, Oh what a guy. He says
he's 35 years old and he lives by himself. He also ask me if
I like to drink. I said once in a while. Then he said you like
wine or beer. And he wanted to bring some beer over to my
place he said he wants to get to know me. Boy what is going
on here. hah! hah!

I said I think it's kind of late right now. So he said he'll
give me a call tomorrow again. Excuse me again the phone is
ringing again. Oh well I am back again Daisy it's another
guy he ask me what I need. I said a couch you know. He told
me he's got a black & white T.V. and it works well. He said
he is a woodworker and likes to work with his hands, He said

he's 62 years old. So he'll call me tomorrow and bring the
T.V. over for me. I am laughing away here all by myself
about these guys from the calls I have. I didn't think any-
body would call me. I just did that for the kick of it. Proba-
bly the paper was out today. This weekend I went with my girl-
friend and her daughter a place called J.R. Dallas after-
hours Club in Hull Quebec. It was a riot there lots of
people. It opens from 9 pm to 5 am in the morning every night.
But the Beer is so expensive would you believe it's three
twenty five a bottle. Plus two dollars for cover charge and
fifty cents for your coat. You should come to Ottawa and
visit me so that I could take you there. I am sure you would
like it. It's like a disco place more (lights of disco's). I
suppose you're getting ready to come to Toronto now for
Christmas holidays. It's to bad I won't be there. I could have
took you to the corner. Well maybe someday. I am suppose to
go to Toronto for my Doctors appointment for my eyes in
second week of December, But I had changed my mind I am
not going after all. I'll make another appointment, sometime
next year. Oh well Daisy Ill let you go for now.

I hope to hear from you real soon. Have a very Merry
Xmas and the New Year coming.
I hope you enjoy yourself.
from (Mini)

It wasn't until after Christmas that Minnie got around to actively
seeking out employment. Each morning she would rise early, don

her coat and boots, and head down to the corner newspaper box. Anxious to see what was new in the classified section, she would rush home, spread the paper out on the kitchen table, and grab her magnifying glass to help her make out the small print. When she spotted a job for which she felt suitable, she would circle the notice, wondering each time how a person that needed a magnifying glass to read the newspaper would handle an interview.

Her acceptance into the Salvation Army's Salem program, which provided occupational training to recovering alcohol and drug abusers, was just the opportunity Minnie needed to get back on her feet. So was her job placement at the Dalhousie Health and Community Services Centre, which was a conveniently short bus ride from her Lowrey Street flat. There, she was responsible for performing secretarial work, counselling, cleaning, running errands—whatever needed to be done.

Minnie enjoyed the little bit of authority she exercised at the centre, approaching simple tasks, such as handing out food stamps and bus tickets, with greater seriousness than the average worker. She viewed the homeless and underprivileged clients of the centre as customers in the true sense—worthy of respect and deserving of the best service possible.

For the average worker, the tasks Minnie performed would have been mundane, but she never regarded them that way. She knew how important the centre's services were to someone who was new to the city, on their own, and without money or a place to sleep. She always managed to slip in a few words of advice between directions: "Get out and meet people." "If you stay in your room you'll go crazy." "Don't blow your cheque in one night." "Don't let strangers get you down." If the clients were native, she made them promise to drop into the Friendship Centre.

Minnie quickly became popular with co-workers Sherry Halgerson and Sandra Barnaby. Both women had met people from programs like Salem who were unable to cope with the stress of seeing people like themselves all day long. They were inspired by

Minnie's ability to remain cheerful despite the troubled faces, scarred lives, and desperate stories that confronted her every day. It was obvious to both of them that Minnie must have borne great pain in her forty years to be able to identify so quickly with the suffering souls she encountered at the centre.

Recognizing that her employment was short-term and that she should take this opportunity to learn from people with university degrees and college diplomas in social work, Minnie approached each new challenge with eagerness. But at the same time, she was cognizant of the fact that no amount of book-smarts could bestow on the other workers the experiences that life had heaped on her.

Her sensitivity, together with a positive attitude and a rabid sense of humour, served Minnie well at the centre. Staff and clients alike loved being in her company; it was common to see seven or eight people hovering around her desk, sitting on it or on the floor next to it, everyone talking at once. On days that she had received a package full of beadwork and moccasins crafted by her mother, the circle of people around her would grow even larger.

Despite her attachment to the centre, Minnie's greatest preoccupation was not her job, but her desire to have her youngest daughter come live with her.

Even without a job, she had tried to talk her mother into letting her bring Violet, first to Toronto ten years before, then to Ottawa this year. But the iron-willed Maggie wouldn't hear of it. The city, she insisted, is no place for a young girl with no family around her and a mother with a drinking problem who can't support herself. Given the choice, Maggie would want all her kids to live the kind of life she and Bart had lived when the children were young: fishing every day for dinner, making clothing and jewellery to sell, and journeying into the bush now and then to make sure you "don't forget who you are."

Minnie couldn't convince her mother that, perhaps, with Violet there, she would have the incentive to secure a steady job and maybe quit drinking once and for all. But her mother wasn't willing to take a chance where her grandchild's well-being was concerned and used as winning counter-arguments, Minnie's failings, along with her own distaste of the way natives who lived in the city were treated.

Minnie's three-month assignment at the centre slipped by quickly. At the end of June 1988, the funding from Salem stopped, prompting the centre to dip into its own slim pockets to keep Minnie on for the summer.

Perhaps it was her naivete, or denial of the prospect of losing something so intrinsically linked with her sense of purpose that left Minnie devastated at the end of the summer when news came: there was no more money to keep her on.

During her last days at the centre, Minnie chose not to burden anyone with her feelings, though she was clearly troubled and the thick lenses that once magnified warmth projected only sadness now. After she stopped working, she continued to visit regularly, each time bringing new people, mostly natives, who needed help. As the weeks passed, her visits became less frequent. Finally, people at the centre just didn't see her anymore.

❧

"I guess we won't be meeting any men tonight," Minnie sighed dramatically. Evelyn was extracting particular enjoyment from Minnie's jokes about not having a date this New Year's Eve and about all the good-looking Vietnamese men up the road in Chinatown just waiting to meet her. Knowing that Minnie was infatuated with Asian men, Evelyn teased her about what it might be like tonight at one of the big Chinese restaurants on Somerset Street: there was sure to be someone there who would catch her fancy.

In good humour, the two women commiserated over spending New Year's Eve alone. They recalled past Christmases and New

Year's Eves. Minnie quipped that travelling down memory lane was as far as either of them would get that night.

She asked Evelyn what she had bought her children for Christmas this year, a form of torture she subjected herself to, not only for not having any money to buy her own daughters gifts this year, but also for not challenging her mother's insistence that she not send Violet presents.

Evelyn started telling Minnie about what some of the clubs in Vanier had planned for New Year's Eve, and wondered aloud who might be there that either of them would know. But Minnie said that, even if she had the money, she wasn't in the mood to go to a bar. What she really wanted to do this New Year's Eve was watch the midnight fireworks display on Parliament Hill.

Chapter Three
CLAUDE'S

*I only got to know Minnie after I came
to Ottawa. Our house was near hers in
Kash, but she wasn't there very much.*
— JOYCE WESLEY

An hour later, bundled in a long brown coat, a woollen scarf wrapped around her neck, and a knitted tuque pulled low to protect her ears from the cold, Minnie arrived at Evelyn's doorstep in Vanier. The moment her old friend opened the door, Minnie's face broke into one of the big smiles that was all too uncommon lately; one that lit up her entire face and almost caused her bifocals to fall off.

Once there, Minnie discovered that Evelyn had invited her friend, Suzie, to tag along to see the fireworks. Suzie was expecting her regular babysitter's sister to arrive "any minute now," and then she would be right over. Minnie removed her coat and boots for the wait.

The two women spent a good hour waiting for Suzie to arrive. During that time, Minnie checked her watch repeatedly; the late hour prompted her to dress and undress several times. Gloves on and tuque in hand, she paced Evelyn's hallway, finally getting too warm and stripping off her coat. Minutes later, she was up performing the same ritual again.

Minnie had reason to worry about the time. The fireworks were scheduled for midnight; it was ten forty-five now, and they still had to walk five blocks to wait for a bus that would take them to Parliament Hill.

Observing Minnie's anxiety heighten as the time passed, Evelyn reminded her that both of them could well have been spending the evening alone. The gentle admonition brought back the empty feeling that Minnie had experienced earlier in the day. Evelyn was right, Minnie thought, though she didn't feel like admitting it right now. She *was* glad to be with her old friend, and even happier to be away from Mechanicsville, which, except for the Elmdale House, a dingy bar up on Wellington, would be dead tonight.

Suzie called shortly before eleven o'clock; her babysitter had just arrived. Since she lived just around the corner from the Claude Tavern, and there was a bus stop right across the street, she suggested they meet there. If she arrived before Evelyn and Minnie, she would wait for them inside, at the bar.

The Claude Tavern—Claude's to its friends—was one of the many taverns hunkered along the stretch of Beechwood that started at the St. Patrick Street bridge and ended at the cemetery that dominated Vanier's easternmost limits. Some fifty years old in 1988, the Claude Tavern thrived as a watering hole for the working class. Newer bars had opened in the area in recent years, and had become popular as well, but not with the sort of people that frequented Claude's.

On a weekend night at Claude's, you could be passed out over the back of your chair, slivers of brown glass sprinkled through your hair, and blood welling from cuts, and still catch the eye of one of the women across the bar. You could curse the English and the Jews, then bust up the table with the help of one of them. Eventually, it would all end nicely, usually over a chuckwagon and a bet on whose father was the meaner bastard. That was life in a place where a day's drudgery could be forgotten for the price of a beer and, regardless of the season, loneliness could be checked at the door like a heavy coat.

The building that housed the Claude Tavern would not have caught the eye of even the most observant passer-by were it not for the reflective orange siding that cut across the top of one full side of the grey stucco exterior. Upstairs were hotel rooms; on the ground level, the tavern consisted of two large rectangular rooms served by a common bar. You entered the ladies-and-escorts side on Maisonneuve Street off Beechwood; you could duck into, and sneak out of, the men's tavern from the parking lot about fifty feet farther back.

A good many of Claude's patrons were regulars, and though their financial circumstances stood in stark contrast, the employed and unemployed customers at Claude's bonded easily.

The employed among Claude's regulars were the type that searched high and low for work—sometimes balancing two and three different jobs in a week—and who only had time between work and home to pop in for a quick beer. These men were supporting wives who were pregnant a good deal of the time, and a large brood of children that, by the time they reached eighteen, were bringing babies of their own home for *grand-mère* to mind. Those who had no jobs or families would hang around the tavern for hours on end, running errands for the staff, listening to other customers' problems, and keeping the place alive with their comings and goings. They lived off welfare, some taking permanent residence in the rooms upstairs.

Before the evening ended, the police would visit and at least one or two people would be tossed out for getting into a rumble. But this would hardly be regarded as a disturbance; an evening without a fight or two would be an off-night, especially frowned upon by those who had the habit of falling asleep and who counted on the occasional wake-up to order another beer.

Last call would be announced close to one a.m. By then smoke would be lowering over the grimy room in a thick cloud that wouldn't dissipate until the following morning when the windows and doors were opened, the terrazzo floors hosed down, and every square inch of the place sprayed with Lysol. The customers would be long dispersed by then. Some would end up in the hotel rooms upstairs; some would simply go home; one or two might spend the night in doorways or apartment foyers along Beechwood. The next night, or the one after that, they would come back to Claude's: an escape for the working man who got up at five in the morning to lay bricks or sweep streets; a magnet for others who hung miserably loose most of the day.

Minnie and Evelyn arrived at the Claude Tavern late that evening–around eleven-fifteen. The place was already full, but that didn't matter; it was New Year's Eve, the people seemed nice, and as soon as the two women appeared, people started to move chairs and partners to make room for them to pass by. One of the men seated at a full table rose to offer his chair to Minnie, prompting another man to offer his to Evelyn. Within minutes of their arrival, a tall Inuit man from Frobisher Bay appeared out of nowhere and offered to buy the table of strangers a round. His name was Sam.

That's when Minnie spotted her two cousins, Joyce and Pauline, across the room at another table near the exit door. They were arguing.

Pauline had just returned to Joyce's table after having been thrown out of the tavern. Apparently, two men had plunked themselves down between the two women, who had been deep in conversation. Pauline had responded to the men by smashing a beer bottle over the head of the fellow closest to her, prompting one of the waiters to pull her out of her chair, grip one arm, and lead her out the front door. When she managed to sneak back in–through the back door–she noticed that Joyce was now alone at the table, quietly contemplating her beer.

At first the two sisters stared at each other without speaking, then Pauline started talking about their other sister, Delma, who had died, together with her three children when their house in Fort Albany had caught fire a few months earlier. As Pauline brought up painful memories about Delma, Joyce's anger mounted. She hadn't come to Claude's this New Year's Eve to talk about the pain their family had suffered throughout the past year. Finally, when Pauline started whining about not being treated fairly as a child, Joyce rose from the table and threw her against the wall. Pauline tore off crying, this time out the back door, leaving Joyce alone again at the table.

Not long after, Joyce spotted Minnie and Evelyn across the room. At first she was reluctant to join them. She had met Evelyn only once, and as for Minnie, Joyce had only gotten to know her cousin since she had arrived in Ottawa a few months before. But she wasn't having any fun alone at her table. She kept getting fearful looks from men who thought she would emulate her departed drinking partner and smash beer bottles over their heads.

She got up, grabbed her coat and beer, and went over to join Minnie and Evelyn.

Coroner's Inquest Testimony – Joyce Wesley

A. This was just before the countdown–countdown of New Year's Eve that I noticed Minnie and Evelyn Mark and two other people sitting in the way far corner by the washrooms, so I was sitting alone at that table and what I did is I took my coat, my beer, and I went to go join them.

Q. So it was an accidental meeting as such.

A. Yes.

Q. You didn't expect to...

A. No, I didn't...

Q. ...be running into her.

A. ...expect to see her there until I saw her there.

Q. And you saw Minnie with Evelyn Mark?

A. Yes.

Q. And who's Evelyn Mark?

A. Her friend.

Q. Her friend? And there was somebody else there with them?

A. Yeah, two other people, a male and a female.

Q. And do you know them at all?

A. No.

Q. And what did you notice about Minnie at this time? What was she doing?

A. Well, she had a beer, like, everybody had a beer in there and...

Q. Um-hmm.

A. ...like, all we did we—we had a good time. We were talking to each other, dancing.

The country-and-western band Select had started its third set just after eleven-thirty. Knowing that the next time they left the stage, it would be a brand-new year, the band members made their entrance all the more dramatic. Dressed for the occasion in their best clothes, they fit in with the guests, but still appeared awkward, as if at any moment they would be transported back to the jamboree.

Lead singer Kelly Madore made her way through the crush toward the planked stage, her heels sticking to the floor as she moved along. Ginette, the guitarist and back-up singer, and Carl, the drummer, followed closely behind. A string of catcalls and clapping welcomed Kelly as she climbed onto the stage. The group started with a few ballads, then, as midnight drew close, they moved into a plodding version of Steve Wariner's "What I Didn't Do." The house favourite would draw the customers out onto the floor so that she could move into "Old Time Rock'n Roll" and get them all hyped up for the countdown.

Minnie got up to dance with an Asian man who had been

playing pinball over by the wall. Evelyn stayed seated and made small talk with the Inuit man who had joined them at their table. Joyce just sat and drank her beer.

It was New Year's Eve, and the people were nice.

ℰ℘

By eleven-thirty, the place was packed tight. It was so crowded that Tom, the Claude Tavern's bartender since the late 1960s, had already been forced several times to leave his post behind the bar and tell groups of people about to take off their coats that they had better look for a New Year's Eve party elsewhere. "Try the Butler," he told at least five disappointed groups of celebrants, knowing that a suggestion to try one of the newer, trendier bars in the area would fall on deaf ears.

The regular bouncer had asked for the night off; when Tom didn't agree, he just didn't bother to appear. Then the replacement offered by the Manpower Agency on Montreal Road didn't show up. Finally, one of the guests suggested that he take a shot at it, assuring Tom that he'd had lots of experience dealing with troublemakers, particularly during his stint in the penitentiary. He started on the job around eight o'clock and by midnight was well on his way to inviting everyone on the street who passed by to come in. The only problem was, he couldn't count and had let some fifty more people through the doors than what fire regulations permitted.

Though Tom kept a wary eye on his new—and temporary—staff member at the front door, he had little time to notice who was queuing up outside, let alone what was going on across the room. His eyes surveyed the room, seeking out people calling for more drinks. As the minutes raced toward the countdown, he became increasingly anxious and issued orders to his waiters to "get those drinks out." He knew that afterwards the orders would remain steady for a while, but closing time would be upon them before they knew it, and that would be it for another year.

Cecil Thomas knew the drill all too well, logging in 1988 as his twenty-second New Year's Eve at the Claude Tavern. No one knew him by his real name; he always went by Tom, which was not an abbreviation for Thomas but rather Tomahawk, the nickname he had picked up twenty years earlier when he played hockey "harder and rougher" than any of his teammates.

Most of the regulars regarded Tom as the proprietor, arranging with one another to "meet at Tom's," or "have a few quarts with Tom." The popular image of him being in charge matched Tom's own perception of himself. Owners came and went, he often said, but a place like Claude's needed someone to *run* it.

Tom took pride in his tavern and always called Claude's a family bar, a place where friends could congregate, where nobody was lonely. It infuriated him when people referred to it as a dump and acted as if the place was beneath them. It also upset him when one of the waiters got rough with a customer. Sure, there were times when you couldn't help but lose your temper, but in his twenty-one years at Claude's, Tom had been in only four fights and had been hurt just once. That was the time a buddy of his broke his nose on a bet so he could get off the hook for paying a one-hundred-dollar debt.

Tom was particularly vigilant over the way the waiters treated the Indian and Inuit customers. Whether it was an affinity to his own nickname or his conviction that the entire country belonged to natives in the first place, Tom always took the time to build a rapport with these shy, quiet individuals who wandered in. He was fascinated by the names of towns he had never heard of, like Iqaluit, Inuktatuk, and Waswanipi, and even more so by the stories of how people survived in such remote places. Tom was also moved by how these customers opened up after a few visits and became ardent conversationalists. He took heart in the belief that Claude's was the right antidote for the apparent loneliness that these people, being new to the city and all, felt.

Natives had only started coming to the Claude Tavern—in significant numbers, that is—in the mid-1980s, when the place was gaining a reputation as a dingy, smoke-filled bar that served cheap draft. Their appearance coincided with the increase in native people leaving their reserves for a better life in the city, only to find in their corner of the urban scene a squalor not that different from what they had left behind.

At Claude's, they congregated in one area, usually at one or two tables. The men loved to drink—beer mostly; so did the women, though most nights there would only be one or two women among a group of about a dozen men. For the most part, their acquaintance with one another was superficial. Even so, they greeted each other warmly and with respect. In a bar, that meant buying drinks for the entire table. At least one person in the group would have money, and if it was the last week in the month, when the welfare cheques came in, all of them would.

A few of the native customers became regulars, showing up every weekend, if not every night. When one of them got rowdy, Tom would insist that he or she calm down or leave. The guest would be ready to argue at first, but would usually accept Tom's argument: "I've got a job to do." If that ploy failed and the guest didn't calm down, Tom would simply walk over and mumble a few unintelligible words in the person's ear. Most times, the troublemakers would quietly down their beers and make their way out without a fuss.

This New Year's Eve, Tom was taking personal pride in the turnout. He had banked on a big crowd, and had gone out with Kelly Madore earlier in the day to get balloons to hang from the fan lights, a couple of hundred gold and green party hats to hand out, some horns with feathers for the countdown, and some after-Christmas-sale artificial poinsettias—one for each table.

They had spent a good two hours that morning getting the room spruced up and it was worth it. All the regulars were there, and those who weren't regulars had arrived sober enough to want to spend lots of money. It didn't appear as if any fights were brewing either; though on New Year's Eve brawls rarely erupted until after the countdown, when the excitement and tension that had built up all evening had to find an outlet.

Tom felt confident that they were all going to sail into '89 without incident.

ॐ

In the last minutes of 1988, the Claude Tavern looked like most other bars on the occasion of ringing in a new year. People were sitting, standing, leaning over packed tables, knocking over beer bottles and tipping ashtrays, gesturing absently to make a point, grunting hellos and Happy New Years over the competing sounds of the band and snooker balls in play. The most energetic among the crowd were flying across the dance floor, satin party dresses and polyester suits scratching against each other in antiquated moves like the hustle, the jive, the twist. A group over by the bar was watching Guy Lombardo's New Year's Eve show on the television, where the volume was turned up high enough to be heard by the nearest customers. Amid the vocal clamour, Kelly and the band kept vying for attention on the assumption that someone actually wanted to hear them, but the steady pinging of the pinball machines was all the acknowledgement they received.

ॐ

Minnie told Joyce the same thing she had told everyone that night, that she and Evelyn were leaving to see the fireworks on Parliament Hill as soon as Evelyn's friend Suzie arrived. Joyce expressed some scepticism; it was almost midnight—they would never make it there on time.

"Besides, you're having a good time here," one person at the table told her. "Why bother standing out in the cold."

Minnie considered their arguments. She had already started to doubt that a bus would get them to the fireworks on time. And if anyone at the table did have a car, they certainly weren't in any condition to drive it.

While her disappointment was visible, Minnie didn't want to make Evelyn feel responsible for Suzie not showing up. Also disappointed, Evelyn echoed her own earlier sentiments: "Well, it's better than staying in," which made Minnie think once again about the apartment that had led to such high hopes in the beginning, but in which she had spent all too much time lately.

By midnight, Minnie had forgotten that she and Evelyn were waiting for anything other than the countdown at Claude's. Good thing, too, because Suzie never showed up.

୫ର

Nineteen eighty-nine arrived with little fanfare. Above the racket, Kelly Madore screeched out the last thirty seconds of the countdown. There were the usual toasts, hugs, and kisses for everyone at your table, and long embraces and loud verbal exchanges out on the floor. Some of the balloons hanging especially low over the tables popped, mostly from lit cigarettes poked at them. People blared horns in other people's faces. Kelly, Ginette, and Carl started up "Auld Lang Syne"; Ginette was standing far back and joined in with extra vocals part-way through when she realized that no one could hear Kelly. Some of the customers near the stage sang a few bars before sashaying onto the dance floor, which was starting to fill again now that the big moment had passed. Tom hollered at one of the waiters to "get those glasses filled," and Sam, the Inuit man at Minnie's table, echoed Tom's order and bought everyone another round.

Tom announced last call just before one o'clock, but no one paid attention; everyone was having too good a time to worry about one voice in the crowd, let alone to think about the night being over. That was okay. Tom knew that the place would stay open late—it always did on New Year's Eve—and any cops that might come in would be off duty and looking for a beer themselves.

He told himself that it couldn't have been a better night: a sign of the year to come. There had been no fights to speak of, and nearly all the kegs stockpiled in the back were empty.

Coroner's Inquest Testimony – Joyce Wesley

A. Before we left, I asked Minnie that, "Let's go down to J.R.'s," but she told me that she didn't have no money and I told her, well, never mind then, if you don't have no money. At that time, an Inuit guy was there, his name was Sam.

Q. An Inuit guy?

A. Yes.

Q. Um-hmm.

A. And—and before we were leaving, he said, "Let's go down to J.R.'s. I'll pay your taxi and I'll pay your booze," so all three of us said O.K. so he called a taxi and we went.

The Claude Tavern began to empty all at once, around one-thirty. Knowing that the competition for taxis out front would be vicious, Sam rushed out—Minnie, Evelyn and Joyce in tow. Sam managed to push his way through the crowd outside and stood in the middle of Beechwood. Almost instantly he flagged down a taxi amidst the torrent of cars zipping by in both directions. He hopped into the front seat next to the driver, who then made a U-turn and stopped in front of Claude's. As the others piled into the back seat, each one of them gave Sam a congratulatory slap on the shoulder.

The party crossed the St. Patrick Street bridge and took the shortcut toward the bridge to Hull. As they passed King Edward Street near the Shepherds of Good Hope hostel, they noticed a crowd on the corner; some of the people were watching the cars speed by, others were putting their rehabilitation from drugs or alcohol on hold for the night. *That's okay, the next three hundred and sixty-five days were going to be hard enough.*

The taxi cruised past the shimmering glass tower that marked the National Gallery of Canada and started the curving descent beneath Nepean Point. As the gallery disappeared above them, the lights of Hull across the river abruptly leapt into view. As they crossed the Alexandra Bridge, Minnie looked over her shoulder to catch a glimpse of Parliament Hill, the detail of its buildings lost to the night. So many native people regarded these buildings as symbols of oppression, each spire a formidable opponent. The people she had come to view as friends in Ottawa looked upon the same buildings as monuments to the idea of freedom, each arch a doorway to opportunity. This New Year's morning, all Minnie knew for sure was that there wouldn't be another major fireworks display until Canada Day, six months down the road.

Chapter Four
LAST CALL

I had worked that evening and got back quite late...Patrick and Michel were asleep and I said, 'Are you guys going to get up?' and they were kind of lazy and I said, 'Come on, it's like eleven-thirty. Let's go to Hull for last call.' So by the time we got there, trying to get a taxi to Hull on New Year's Eve...it was pretty late.

— DAVID KNOX, Student

The city of Hull, Quebec, has a traditional link with Ottawa. The west Quebec city of about one hundred thousand predominantly French-speaking people lies directly across the Ottawa River from Canada's capital. In the early years of European settlement, the feuding English and French inhabitants north and south of the river paid homage to the waterway's importance and to the Adawa band of Algonquian Indians who traded at the site. Both adopted versions of the native word for it: the French called it Outaouais; the English, Ottawa. Old Bytown, the unofficial capital of English Canada, went one step further, claiming the river as its own and renaming the city Ottawa as well.

In the decade before Confederation in 1867, Ottawa became the capital of a supposedly united English and French Canada. By then, cultural and language differences between the two peoples who claimed Canada as their own were entrenched in the public consciousness, making Ottawa and Hull official, yet often bitter, neighbours.

Hull shares with Ottawa what most English-speaking Canadians call the National Capital Region, which means that more than just the city of Ottawa gets a share of federal tax dollars to look presentable. Most national, and local, events include Hull in more than a tokenistic way. Dressing up Ottawa means dressing up Hull for events like Canada Day and the Tulip Festival, a visit by a foreign dignitary, and those occasions on which Canada hosts a summit of world leaders.

In the 1960s, Ottawa and Hull were brought into a hasty union, mostly to prepare for the 1967 Canadian Centennial celebration. The marriage delighted federalists in the parent provinces of Ontario and Quebec, but it rode roughshod over the separate identities of the two cities. It also ignored the distinct physical character of each city for the sake of what many believed was an uncertain future.

Rather than commemorate the buildings that had been there for most of the hundred years being celebrated, Ottawa's city council ratified an agreement to tear them down—some of the best ones anyway—and approved the construction of contemporary office towers.

Hull fell victim to the same metamorphosis that gripped Ottawa in preparation for the Centennial celebration. Most of the old buildings along the waterfront were torn down to make way for the government office towers that were to make Hull more than an incidental part of the nation's capital.

But while Ottawa laid claim to the part of Hull that it had to look at every day, it was never able to change the heart and culture of the old mill town. Especially Promenade du Portage, the boulevard known to people in Hull as rue Principale; visitors from the Ontario side of the river called it *the strip*.

The strip runs from Eddy Street, named after the E. B. Eddy Paper Company that has resided there for some 150 years, to rue Laurier, where it curves to meet the same plant's east-end fine paper mill. Just four blocks long, the strip has hosted as many as twenty bars at one time, interspersed with restaurants, pizza parlours, a couple of hotels, and a boarded-up cinema that once showed adult films. To distinguish one bar from the next, proprietors have traditionally erected gargantuan neon signs that have taken the exaggerated forms of lipstick tubes and palm trees, and have proclaimed the exclusivity of their establishments by giving them names such as Zap and J. R. Dallas, names that tended to change every year or two, sometimes along with the owners.

Amidst the vast array of nightclubs stood the true landmark of the strip—an intersection nicknamed the Four Corners because of its size in relation to the narrow streets that funnel into it. There, in the early hours of the morning, cars would make turns off the strip onto rue Laval, then line up to cross the bridge to Ottawa. On its median, dozens of people in groups of three and four, would stand and wave down taxis, often to no avail. On the strip, after the bars closed, neither cars nor pedestrians had much immediate success in going anywhere.

❦

In 1988, the dance bars and taverns in Hull and throughout Quebec were open until three o'clock in the morning, giving people from across the river in Ontario a place to go after the bars there closed at one a.m. But people came to Hull for more than an extra hour or two of drinking. They came to experience that *other* culture, the one they paid lip-service to sharing, but in reality considered foreign.

Despite assertions to the contrary, the relationship between the inhabitants of Ottawa and Hull have always been strained: in vying for government jobs; in determining which language to start a conversation with; in celebrating separately the occasions the two cities are supposed to be sharing. But at three a.m. on the strip, people are generally too tired, too drunk, or too anxious for sex to worry about "them and us," and saying the right things. They are there to have a good time: dancing inside one of the bars until it closes; in a restaurant wolfing down hamburgers and club sandwiches; outside a pizza place sharing slices among friends. If not in a bar or at a food stop, they are out on the street watching hot bodies slide by, congregating in the middle of the road to jeer at cars, or musing with friends about why the cops look so mean when everyone is having such a good time.

The cab dropped Minnie and her friends off just east of J. R. Dallas, where a service lane left an opening in the tall snowbank that covered half the sidewalk. Sam marched up to the door under the bright sign—a cowboy hat lit by fluorescent bulbs—and pulled out his wallet to pay for all of them to get in. They had just got their hands stamped and were on their way into the main room when the bouncer blocked Sam.

They had been having such a good time at Claude's that no one had noticed the way Sam was dressed, let alone told him he couldn't get into J.R.'s wearing construction boots. It was also the first time that night that they wondered who Sam really was and why he didn't know the standard bar policies, especially when he could drink with the best of them.

Trying to make the best of what was left of the night, they decided to leave with Sam. After all, he had made good for the cab and had already paid for them to get into J.R.'s. It wouldn't have been right to just leave him there alone with nowhere to go. Not on New Year's Eve.

Coroner's Inquest Testimony – Joyce Wesley

A. So, when we knew that he couldn't go in, we went—over to Zap's to go try it there and the same thing happened there, they couldn't let him in.

Q. It's not part of the dress code to wear steel-belted boots. Like construction boots.

A. That's right.

Standing in front of Zap in the cold and feeling the chill of rejection, they gave up hope that Sam would get in anywhere with those boots. They headed back toward J.R.'s, discussing, while they walked, what to do next. Then Sam was gone. They stopped and looked around, but a group of people were at their heels, irritated at the halt in the flow of pedestrian traffic and visibly anxious to get somewhere before closing time.

Just as well. Their stamps still fresh on their palms, Minnie, Joyce, and Evelyn made their way back to J.R.'s half an hour before it closed.

J. R. Dallas opened in 1981, one of hundreds of bars across North America to tip their stetsons to the popular television show "Dallas" and its charismatic tycoon, formidable oilman J. R. Ewing. A combination saloon and dance bar, J.R.'s was a place where, eighteen years of age or fifty, drinker or not, a visitor could always enjoy a surfeit of country music and a fair share of casual conversation. The big square space was decorated with saddles hitched to the walls and wagon wheels hanging from the ceiling. A long rustic bar ran the length of the room. To the left was the dance floor, its parquet tiles sprinkled with sawdust kicked across from the rest of the room. Surrounding the dance floor were tables, occupied mostly by people in their thirties and forties, talking, but not loud enough to drown out the musical wailings of Alabama reverberating from speakers on either side of the dance floor. A dozen or so stools lined a counter that ran along the back wall to meet the far end of the bar; in front of these sat a few more tables surrounded by four or five chairs each. If you had advanced this far into J.R.'s you were in the *Indian section*.

Coroner's Inquest—Cross-Examination – Joyce Wesley

Q. O.K. In J. R. Dallas's, you said that you were in the Indian section?

A. Yes.

Q. Could you explain that to me, what you mean by Indian section?

A. Well... when the Indians go there to go drink, like, they go to the back bar. That's where most Indians go, to the back bar. That's why they call it the Indian section.

Q. I see. And the other people go to the front bar?

A. Well, at the Indian section, some white people will be there, yeah.

Q. Uh-huh.

A. And on the—on the other bar, on the other side, like, some Indians will go also to the other bar.

Q. O.K. But they refer to the back bar as the Indian section.

A. Yes.

Q. Then a lot of Indians drink at J. R. Dallas's?

A. I think so.

Q. O.K. Have you been there before?

A. A couple of times.

The Indian section was a popular spot with natives who had left their reserves to come to Ottawa, and who migrated to open-all-night restaurants and country bars around town. Even if they had never met before and were from different tribes, or different bands of the same tribe, they talked about how things were going, who was new in town, the music the deejay was playing, and when the song one of them had requested would play.

Nearly all of the Indians in town—some of the Inuit, too—liked the atmosphere of a country bar, mostly for the music. The straightforward lyrics of the songs plumbed the essence of their longing for homes they could never manage to stick with, and eased some of the pain they suffered when made to feel unwelcome in a new one.

At J.R.'s most of the people came in lonely and left lonely, but found companionship while they were there. On this New Year's Eve, the natives in J.R.'s appeared to be having such a good time that a whole table of whites—*amistickooshoo*—from across the room had picked up their drinks and brought them over to the Indian section to join in the fun.

$\gg$

One would never have guessed the late hour by the number of people still inside J.R.'s. Sure, some people were putting their coats on. Others, mostly women, were pulling at their partners' arms, coaxing them to skip another drink. But despite everyone's best efforts, or intentions, few people in J.R.'s were actually on their way out.

Minnie ignored any signals of an exodus and breezed in as if she owned the place, giving hugs and kisses to acquaintances standing over by the entrance. She stopped to chat at tables on the far side of the dance floor, then made her way over to the Indian section where she recognized three women she knew from The Well, a support centre for women in need. Evelyn followed; when she spotted two friends, Sean and Fred, she sat down at their table. Joyce, knowing fewer people at J.R.'s than Minnie or Evelyn, staggered over to the other side of the room.

$\gg$

Since early the previous day, Joyce had been determined to make the best of her night on the town. With a working husband and three children, she rarely went out, except to bingo, and shied away from social interaction with people outside her family. She was one of nineteen children, fourteen of whom were still alive. In a culture in which the extended family is central to its value system, she was kept busy with a husband, children, brothers and sisters; she had little time or interest in cultivating other relationships. Though Minnie was her cousin, their only common experience was that both had lived in a house in Kashechewan that had running water, a privilege shared by only a third of families living on the reserve. During the times that both women were in Kash at the same time, they would greet one another when they met at the Northern store, but rarely had much to talk about except children and weather. Then, they might share a few words and a chuckle over how expensive healthy food, like fruits and vegetables, was on the reserve, while Coke and chips could be had for a steal.

This New Year's Eve, they had had something else in common—a dismal chance of going out. Joyce had tried for the past two weeks to get a babysitter, but it wasn't easy to find one for that night, especially when you didn't have the means to pay very much. For days, her husband, Billy, had been coaxing her to go out with one of her sisters—she hadn't been out with anyone but him in such a long time—but the more he encouraged her, the guiltier she felt. He practically had to push her out the door, which at first really provoked her, because she felt he had as much right to go out as she did. But remembering how depressed she had been lately, and how it had been affecting their relationship, Joyce realized that spending the evening apart would probably be good for both of them.

❧

When last call was announced, the three women were just getting started, each having her own brand of fun. Evelyn was listening to the stories flowing round the table where she drank with Sean and Fred. Joyce, one of the tallest women in J.R.'s, stood over a table across the room, where a white man—half her size it seemed—kept insisting that she sit down at a chair he had just pulled over from another table. Minnie was downing a beer while holding court with the women from The Well and a few male acquaintances. She chattered about missing the fireworks, then started to tell the kind of jokes that everyone expected of her. She spotted an Asian man across the dance floor and cast a demure smile that made her friends laugh, then went on to describe, in detail, a fantasy that involved the man with whom she was enraptured. Everyone around her became hysterical when she pointed to Joyce, who could barely stand and who appeared ready to topple an entire table, including the man she was speaking with.

Police Statement – *Joyce Wesley*
She will indicate that while at J. R. Dallas...she along with Minnie Sutherland and other acquaintances consumed some alcohol and that at 3:30 a.m. when the bar closed she left with Minnie Sutherland.

Down the strip and up the side roads that climbed away from it, the bars had started to empty, and the sidewalks and streets had begun to swell with people. Police officers stood at each intersection, particularly at the Four Corners, keeping the traffic moving and using firm words and gestures to prevent pedestrian loitering at any one place. The sounds of car horns filled the air, followed by angry exchanges that quickly gave way to passionate greetings. The sound of boots squishing through the slush on the sidewalks mingled with the tap of spike heels piercing the grey, wet layer to reach concrete.

৪৯

Three university students from Ottawa–David Knox, Michel Filion, and Patrick Smith–had just left Le Pub, a bar just off the strip, and were headed west toward Laval. They were glad they had decided to go out, after all. Their idea of sitting out the New Year's Eve festivities for a year, of just having a quiet drink with some close friends, had seemed attractive, in concept. But when the three of them were actually sitting in front of the television in Patrick's apartment, toasting only one another, they had known something was missing.

Le Pub had proven to be the perfect antidote. Like J. R. Dallas, it was one of the less pretentious spots in the area. It had the standard dance floor, but it also had an upstairs level with pool tables, arcade games, and an outdoor terrace. Like the other bars on or close to the strip, it was packed full that night.

Coroner's Inquest Testimony – Michel Filion

A. ...we had two beer in the bar and it was 3:30, because we arrange the same taxi to pick us up at 3:30 at Promenade du Portage where the accident happen.

Q. O.K.

A. Then that's why we left the bar at quarter to three.

Q. Which bar were you at?

A. At The Pub, in Hull.

Q. Is there a specific name for that one or...?

A. No. No, it's up the street by–just not far from Chez Henri.

Q. All right. Is it close to J. R. Dallas or...?

A. No, no...

Q. But it's somewhere in that area.

A. Um-hmm.

Q. All right. And is that all that you had to drink?

A. Yeah.

Q. A glass of champagne around midnight, and then two beers.

A. Two beers, yeah, when I got in Hull.

Q. Are these small or large?

A. Beer?

Q. Yes.

A. They were just normal beer, not the quart or what-ever. Just the normal beer.

Q. All right. Were you using any drugs?

A. No, I wasn't.

Q. All right. Were you intoxicated in any way?

A. No. No.

When the three men reached the intersection at Laval, they peered into the windows of each of the eight or ten cabs in the street, hoping to spot the driver who had brought them over and who had promised to be back at three-thirty, sharp. They discussed the possibility that the driver had already picked up another fare in Ottawa, or that he was adhering to the rule that disallowed Ottawa cabs from picking up fares in Hull.

They started walking again, tired and ready to go home but, at the same time, intrigued by the endless stream of people flowing out of the bars on the busy part of the strip west of Laval. As they crossed Laval, they realized that they were among dozens of people at the intersection, frantically waving their arms in pursuit of cabs, pleading with those who had successfully hailed one to let them tag along. Beyond the intersection, they noticed a single mass of people in the road that separated J.R.'s and the General Trust Building. They quickened their pace thinking that they might be better off hailing a cab farther down the strip.

❦

Inside J.R.'s, one of the bouncers had left his post at the door to approach the Indian section, where he told the crowd to start making their way out. A few people got up and left; others, including Evelyn, headed toward the front with their beer in hand.

Minnie was holding a couple of men captive with one of her more lascivious stories, but took a long sip of her beer and gestured to her friends that she was going to follow. Joyce was already in the front section of the bar, drunk enough to follow any one of the people around her who was willing to take the lead.

The three women had not made any plans about how they would get home, or whether they would grab a ride together or separately. Whoever managed to get a cab or a ride from someone would take the others if they were within earshot when the opportunity arose. They were all seasoned bar hoppers; none of them particularly worried about how the others would get home. Somehow they would all reach home safely.

✌️

Although Evelyn appeared to leave first, Joyce made it out onto the sidewalk in front of J.R.'s before the others. The air was refreshing after several hours in smoky bars. She ran into a friend, Alan Roper, and his sister, Lise. They invited her to a party in Quebec, but Joyce said she wanted to go home. Then she noticed Sam hanging around outside the boarded-up cinema next to J.R.'s. She slid through a knot of fast-moving people to ask him where he had disappeared to after they left Zap.

Police Statement – *Joyce Wesley*
She will indicate that she was speaking with some friends outside the J. R. Dallas night spot while her cousin Minnie Sutherland proceeded across Place du Portage Street in search of a taxicab or a ride back to Ontario.

Outside J.R.'s, Evelyn decided to join Sean and Fred for a cup of coffee at the Castel, one of two restaurants on the far side of the cinema that abutted J.R.'s. She knew it would be impossible to get a cab while everyone else was trying to get one, and besides, it would be a nice way to end the night. Before she entered the restaurant, she saw Minnie leave the bar and cut through a line of cars in order to cross the road, probably with the aim of waving down a cab. *Good luck*, Evelyn thought.

Part Two

THE MOON

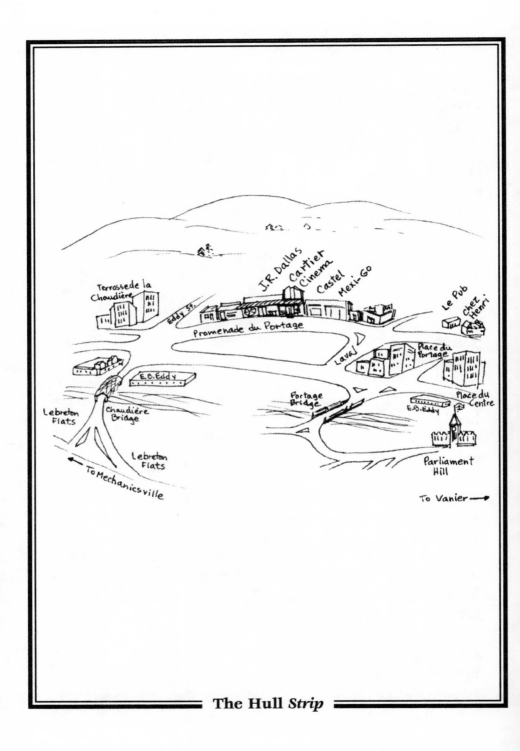

The Hull *Strip*

Chapter Five
HAPPY NEW YEAR

They kept telling us to leave because there was a lot of traffic. They didn't care about her. They didn't even look at her.

– CAROLE ST-DENIS

Three a.m. onward, the doors of the bars along the busiest part of the strip, between Eddy and Laval, dumped tired, intoxicated New Year's Eve celebrants into the streets. Out of the twelve-odd bars in that block alone, a couple of thousand people spilled out, the patrons of one establishment intermingling with those of another as they went in different directions, some shouting for a cab, others heading for the parking lots off the nearest side street.

Out of the clubs they flowed, a customer profile indescribable at every turn. Long torsos in tight skirts followed wide posteriors covered in rhinestones; preppy college students, alternately scratching their heads and their groins, succeeded grungy men venting the pungent aroma of alcohol through gaping holes in their teeth.

They gathered in the street, on the sidewalk—anywhere, really, where a vacant spot of asphalt or concrete accommodated them. They talked and sang, screamed obscenities at one another then laughed about it, and huddled together to keep warm. Most had not been ready to leave the party and, once out on the street, cursed themselves for paying heed to the closing-time announcement while some of their friends were still inside enjoying themselves. Others were too tired to want to stay in the bars, or even outside them. These stood in the crowd peering above the sea of heads to scout out a cab whose back seat might be vacant.

The three or four dozen taxis in the area were navigated through the crush by Lebanese and East Indian drivers, impatient with the traffic and the effect it would have on one of the biggest tipping nights of the year. Eyes focused straight ahead, one hand freed from the wheel and poised to hit the horn, they were intent on making it to the end of the strip as quickly as they could. Once there, they could pick up speed and make up lost time on any of several routes to the city's outlying communities or to Ottawa. Then, after racing those customers home, they could return and pick up another fare. There were never enough cabs for the crowd at this time of the morning on a regular night; on New Year's, stragglers would still be waiting to be collected at dawn.

◈

While the strip, with all its lights, sounds, and people, resembled a carnival midway, the renowned intersection at Laval resembled the street at rush hour. Police officers were occupied on all four corners under tall street lights that blanketed the street in a brilliant canopy of white. Others stood on the median on the section of Laval that started on the south side of the strip. There was little they could do except keep the traffic crawling along at its current snail's pace, and prevent people from following through with spontaneous notions of riding the hood of a car or lying down in the middle of the road.

Coroner's Inquest Testimony – Hull Police Officer Denis Regimbald

Q. Maybe you could just tell us a little bit about the problems that you have as a police officer when it comes to closing time in the bars in Hull.

A. Well, let's say that, at the time of closing of the bars, there are a lot of people on the sidewalks, in the street. They shout. It's an atmosphere–it's a rather very special atmosphere.

Q. O.K. And, in general, is it an atmosphere or, in general, do you have a problem as far as the police are concerned in gaining the respect of the people that are coming out of the bars or are you constantly in conflict with them?

A. There's no conflict that exists there.

Q. Correct me if I'm wrong, but my impression was that you're often given, as police officers, you're often given a difficult time, in particular, by some of the young people that come out of the bars.

A. It's normal, on account of the fact there are all kinds–that there are all kinds of people, there is a lot of people, and certain of these are aggressive and they have less inhibitions.

West of Laval, on the most active part of the strip, there was little to distinguish this night of celebration from any Friday or Saturday night at this hour. In fact, outside J.R.'s, where hundreds of people were gathered, the only hint of a bigger crowd that night was the extreme congestion of what has always been too small an area, and too narrow a road, for the competition between so many vehicles and pedestrians.

Winter never made things easier. By the third or fourth snowfall, the heavy sidewalk traffic always caused the snowbanks to shift onto the road, eliminating the second traffic lane. The passing of the snowplows once a week would help to open the road, but it usually ended up making the snowbanks higher, and, as the winter progressed, icier.

East of Laval, a fight had broken out, but a Hull police cruiser pulled up seconds after it started. The officers who jumped out of the cruiser acted quickly: if they didn't manage the situation adequately, there was always the danger of people taking sides and a mob fight ensuing. Just moments behind the police, an ambulance arrived, and a pack of people, making its way west, suddenly turned back to see if someone was hurt. Before a crowd could form, another cruiser pulled up, and its two officers started ushering people away. Within minutes, pedestrian traffic was on its original course, and the ambulance drove away empty.

Most of the ambulances called to the Hull strip on weekends between midnight and four a.m. return to their posts empty. A busted jaw or a knife in the arm or leg gets everyone worried at first, and the police are obliged to make the call. But concern soon dissipates once the police officers realize that no rival gangs are involved, or that two equally intoxicated buddies just got into a tug-of-war over a girl. Typically, the people involved quickly become preoccupied with distancing themselves and their friends from an arrest, a goal not likely to be achieved by crawling into an ambulance.

Two off-duty nurses from the Ottawa General Hospital, Carole St-Denis and Lorraine DeGrace, were driving west along the strip in Carole's 1980 Pontiac. They had just left the New Year's Eve party at Chez Henri, and were part of a bumper-to-bumper procession proceeding toward Eddy Street.

The Pontiac made the required stop at the Four Corners. Carole waited her turn before proceeding through the broad intersection, then picked up speed. Lorraine made a comment about all the people still out at three-thirty in the morning. She noticed how so many of them were packed tight on the sidewalks, the occasional person forced to climb a snowbank by the sheer pressure of the crowd.

Both women heard a bang on the driver's side of the car. At first, Carole thought someone had run into her from behind, but, as she looked out her side mirror, she could see a person beside her door, sitting in the middle of the road. By the time Lorraine had managed to lean over her friend for a look, the woman in the brown coat and big woollen tuque was lying flat on her back.

There were too many people in the street for much attention to be paid to the woman who had darted through traffic and who now lay on her back next to the blue Pontiac. Only those directly in front of J.R.'s, or the cinema next to it, saw what happened. Others, a bit farther down the strip, heard a thump that could have been anything at that time of the morning. Ten, maybe fifteen, people in the vicinity stopped to look. For a moment, the woman lay motionless; then she started to move her arms and legs. Her head rested flat against the pavement in a tire track, her tuque soaking up water through the slush.

When the incident occurred, Patrick Smith, David Knox, and Michel Filion–the three students who had left Le Pub in search of a cab a half hour before–were standing on the north-west corner of the intersection at Laval. Moments before, Michel had chuckled when he spotted the short, plump figure of a woman lose her balance and slide down a snowbank onto the road, then get up and start crossing the street.

That's when they, too, heard a thump. David pointed and yelled, "Oh my God. . .someone just got hit." He shot off ahead of the others, who followed him to where a figure lay on the ground beside a late-model car that two young women had just leapt out of.

A man jumped out of the clot of people standing on the sidewalk in front of J.R.'s. The hole left by his sudden departure created an opening in the crowd just large enough for Joyce Wesley to have an unobstructed view of what was going on. By now, she was having a hard time holding her head up, let alone focusing on some street musician or fight. But the look on the face of the stranger who had opened the crowd told her that something bad had happened. So did the frantic movements of Michel Filion, who had appeared out of nowhere, waving his arms and screeching "Don't move her, she's been hit by a car." Joyce leaned forward for a better look and saw two other women crouched over someone lying on the road. The big tuque looked familiar, but the absence of eyeglasses made it impossible for Joyce to even guess that the person on the road was Minnie.

Carole St-Denis proceeded to conduct a neurological examination of Minnie, while Lorraine DeGrace took her pulse. Opening Minnie's eyes to check her pupils, Carole instantly noticed the white spots and exclaimed, "Oh, Lorraine, she's blind." She took Minnie's hand and asked her to squeeze her hand. Minnie obliged, and at the same time moved her legs.

Carole looked up from her crouched position to see a tall native woman standing above her, calling, "Minnie, Minnie, Minnie." Carole was about to ask if the tall woman was a friend of the fallen woman but her attention was suddenly drawn to a commotion beyond.

Coroner's Inquest Testimony – Carole St-Denis

A. (Through interpreter)...And there was a guy there, he was all panicky, and he was jumping up and down and he kept repeating, "Call an ambulance, call an ambulance, call an ambulance," and he just wasn't stopping.

Q. All right.

A. This was while Lorraine was looking on. "It's O.K. We're nurses. You go call the ambulance. We'll stay with her." Then he left, and he was supposed to go and call an ambulance.

It was the sudden halting of traffic that made two young police officers patrolling this part of the strip stop their van and get out. They sauntered over, pushing people out of the way and uttering a few calming words as they went. When they made it to the centre of the excitement, they noticed an Indian woman lying on her back, another Indian woman bent over her, and two other women kneeling on the ground next to her. Three young men were standing by the sidewalk talking. One suddenly ran off, yelling over his shoulder that he would call 911. The other two remained: one darted back and forth, stamping his feet into the snow and throwing his arms about; the other watched the fallen woman with concern, looking to her attendants for some diagnosis or direction, trying at the same time to calm his friend down.

Coroner's Inquest Testimony – Michel Filion

A. The police came out of their van, and they didn't really ask what happened and I said–in English, I said, "She just got hit by a car," and I saw they were French, and I said, "Elle s'est fait frapper par une auto, she got hit by the car," and they didn't react, they didn't correspond, they didn't do nothing, and they had a briefly [sic] talk with the nurses, and after that, they say, "Let's keep–let's keep moving, moving the traffic," and they looked at me and say, "Go away, move, move." And I said, "Hey, guys," I said, "she just..."–"Elle s'est fait frapper par une auto, she just got hit by the car..."

Traffic in both directions was at a standstill. On the north side of the street, the cars couldn't pass because Carole's car was stopped where the accident had occurred, right in the middle of the lane. The traffic going the other way was also stopped, partly because of the bottleneck at the Four Corners, but mostly because of the curiosity of those in closest proximity to the action.

The group of pedestrian onlookers on both sides of the street now started to grow, and a few of the people in the cars closest to the Pontiac got out, either to help or to look.

Within seconds of their arrival, the two officers, Denis Regimbald and Guy Vincent, became visibly anxious. It had taken only moments for the cluster of five or six people surrounding the women on the road to grow into twenty, then fifty, curious onlookers. Heads poked out from doorways as bouncers left their gateposts, from apartment windows above the clubs and restaurants, from cars farther down the road that had started continuously honking their horns. Even from afar, all eyes were on that narrow part of the strip outside J. R. Dallas; those in the vicinity who couldn't see what the commotion was all about were certain to hear Michel Filion shouting first in French, "Elle s'est fait frapper par une auto," then in English, "She's just been hit by a car."

The officers started arguing with Michel over who was in charge, you or us, while Michel kept insisting that the woman lying on the road had been hit by a car. Michel's friend Patrick Smith intervened, politely telling the officers that the woman on the ground had been hit by a car and that she shouldn't be moved until an ambulance comes. The information didn't seem to faze either of the officers. *"Let's keep moving–circulez"*–was all they took turns saying.

Michel wouldn't let up, and Patrick's urging him to stop only served to further infuriate him. Officer Vincent bent down over Minnie while Officer Regimbald escorted Michel to the sidewalk in an effort to deal with him as discreetly as possible. Officer Vincent, meanwhile, asked if anyone knew the woman who was on the ground, knowing already that the lady beside her calling "Minnie, Minnie, Minnie" did.

Coroner's Inquest Testimony – Guy Vincent

A. When I crouched near Joyce, at that time I asked her what was happening, if the person lying down was sick and whether she needed an ambulance. She answered me no because she was just under the influence of alcohol, she had fallen and this happened to her frequently while under the influence of alcohol.

Q. Now, did you put that in your statement?

A. I wrote in my statement that she had told me that she was with her, that she was drunk and she had fallen.

Q. O.K. But did you put in your statement that she does that often?

A. No.

Q. O.K. Why not?

A. It's things—when I wrote my statement, it was eight days later, so I wrote in my statement that I remembered in general as to the facts in the statement.

Q. O.K. Because Joyce Wesley has also told us that, even though she admits having a poor memory as to what happened on the night in question, she does, however, maintain that she's never seen Minnie drunk before and she's never drank with her before.

Crouched over Minnie, and temporarily shaken out of her languor, Joyce repeatedly asked her cousin if she was all right. Minnie said she was, and made an effort to try to lift herself. She raised her head but then let it fall gently with the help of Joyce's outreached arms. Carole and Lorraine were still checking her, feeling her pulse, and asking questions to which she kept responding "I'm all right." When Officer Vincent tried to lift Minnie into a sitting position, Michel Filion resumed his tirade about not moving her.

Officer Regimbald had had enough and, in French, ordered Michel to leave: "Va-t'en," he repeated several times, each time more loudly than the last. Patrick grabbed Michel's arm and pulled him onto the sidewalk, telling him to keep quiet before they all got arrested. The officer then joined his partner in lifting Minnie into a sitting position. Despite the initial effect of the officer's words, as well as those of his friend, Michel spoke up again about not moving her; this time Carole St-Denis joined in.

Carole was incensed. Still uncertain about what had actually happened, she knew something wasn't right. Why were the police officers acting so indifferently in the face of an accident where someone was hurt? Did the lady being referred to as "Minnie" walk into her car, or had she hit her? Was Minnie truly all right or had she sustained internal injuries? And where was the ambulance that the English boy had said he was going to call?

Finally, when one of the officers asked Carole three times in succession whether it was her car that was stopped in the road, Carole turned to him, and in an equally trying voice said, "Now, listen here. We want to make sure that she's all right before we leave," explaining that she and Lorraine were nurses. The information had little effect on the officer, who responded firmly, "For the last time, take your car and go."

Carole looked to Lorraine for answers, but Lorraine was equally puzzled. What was going on here? Did the officers know something that they didn't? Perhaps an ambulance was already on its way and the officers wanted them to move their car from its inconvenient position blocking traffic. After all, they were police officers. Maybe this was the way they handled these situations.

Lorraine had another feeling: that the officers knew Minnie. It wasn't that they stumbled upon the incident, sighed, and said something like, *Oh, her again.* It wasn't that obvious. It was just a feeling that Lorraine had. Afterwards, she shared it with Carole, and both agreed that this must be the case.

♔

Now in a sitting position, Minnie looked disoriented; she appeared to be groping for something in the snow. Carole kept looking at her face in an attempt to determine the extent of her injuries, if any. Joyce mumbled something about a pair of glasses, which prompted Lorraine to pick through the slush for them. Patrick stood on the sidewalk next to Michel. Both men looked beyond the collection of voyeurs for any sign of David Knox to confirm that, indeed, help was on the way.

The two police officers walked over to their van for a brief conference, returning seconds later to tell Carole, again, to move her car. They were perplexed by what seemed to be an overreaction to a drunk woman who had either slipped on an ice patch and fallen, or walked into a car that couldn't have been going very fast given all the traffic. They turned to Joyce and asked if she wanted a taxi for herself and Minnie.

Joyce posed the question to Minnie, but without waiting for a response, nodded yes. Officer Regimbald went to the van to place the call. When he came back, David Knox was standing there, out of breath, with the news that Hull didn't have 911 service yet. Both officers insisted once again that Carole move her car. This time she did, wondering as she pulled away why neither of the officers had asked for their names or to see her driver's licence.

Coroner's Inquest Testimony – Joyce Wesley

A. That's when the two cops grabbed her and took her over to the snowbank, dragged her to the snowbank. Before they did that, I was looking for Minnie's glasses and her handbag. She didn't have her glasses on and I didn't know where her handbag was, and when the cops grabbed her, like, I noticed her handbag under her and her glasses. That's where I got them from and they drag–and they dragged her to the snowbank.

Shock registered on the faces of the people watching the officers move Minnie to the side of the road. Bystanders on the sidewalk saw the two officers lift Minnie from under the shoulders, pull her toward the side of the road, and set her down in the snow. Those closer to Minnie saw each officer grab a shoulder of her coat and drag her through the slush, arms dangling limp, heels bumping along the road, and head lolling back and forth, over to the side of the road. They dropped her in the snowbank in front of J.R.'s, the same place where Minnie had begun her search for a ride home a few minutes before.

The numb silence that had overcome the group of onlookers was finally broken by the splash of tires spewing slush as they rolled by. Michel spoke up first, a loud cry about the injustice of not calling an ambulance, of moving a woman who had been hit by a car, and of letting the car that hit her leave the scene.

"What are you doing, guys?" he asked in as reasonable a tone as he could muster. "I told you not to move her."

One of the officers pointed at Michel and warned him about talking to a police officer that way. Michel got angry again and challenged them, but both officers ignored him and walked toward their van.

Joyce collected Minnie's belongings, cleaned off her cousin's purse, and wiped her glasses. David and Patrick moved in to help her. David asked Minnie if she wanted an ambulance but she said no and tried to stand. He offered to help the two women into the restaurant so that they could get off the street, out of the cold, and away from the crowd. The two officers, overhearing these deliberations, returned and asked Joyce if she still wanted the taxi. She looked at Minnie, who still looked disoriented but was trying hard to get up, then at Officer Regimbald, who was impatiently awaiting her answer. David's offer seemed better.

Taped Call to Hull Police Headquarters (Translation of excerpt)

"25 to 46." "Yes, I'm listening." "Cancel the taxi now. The squaw decided otherwise."

Chapter Six
DECISIONS AND DELIBERATIONS

*There were people at The Well who
stood out... Minnie wasn't one of those.
I think she might have wanted to even be
invisible, especially around white people.*
 – KAREN IRVING
Social Worker at The Well

The moment that Hull police officers Regimbald and Vincent began to make their way back to their van, the crowd began to disperse. It was as if a signal had sounded an all-clear assuring everyone that things were normal, that people could resume their well-wishing and be on their way.

In a few minutes, much of the crowd had lost interest in the event and was moving on, too. Patrick Smith was still there, so was Michel Filion, marvelling in his fury at people's indifference, unconvinced that the situation was under control simply because two irresponsible officers declared it so.

David Knox was standing at the side of the road, staring through the widening gaps in the crowd in search of some resolution. Out of the corner of his eye, he could see Joyce. She was bent over Minnie, calling her name repeatedly and pulling at her as if she had just passed out on a dance floor and was embarrassing both of them. She tried to get her to sit up straight, but had little luck: Minnie kept falling, first to one side, then to the other.

David heard the doors of the police van open, then close. He clutched his breast pocket looking for a pen, then called out to a knot of onlookers when he couldn't find one.

Joyce was now trying to pull Minnie into a standing position, but, despite strenuous effort, couldn't shift the good hundred and twenty pounds of dead weight.

David had just finished scribbling down the number of the van when he noticed Joyce lose her balance, which forced her to relinquish her grip on Minnie. He slipped the paper and pen inside his jacket and climbed into the snowbank to assist Joyce by giving Minnie a shove from behind. Patrick also started to lend a hand, but halted when he spotted Michel, whose anger had been rewhetted by the sight of the departing police. Patrick reached him just in time to curb two raised fists and to cap a volcano of ranting about how the officers had handled the situation and what he was going to do about it.

Consumed by uncertainty rather than anger, Joyce and David padded tentatively about, like caged and vulnerable animals, until they were rejoined by Patrick and Michel. Desperate for some kind of privacy, they huddled together for a moment, then lifted Minnie to a standing position.

Minnie's weight was now distributed among the others; her boots dragged through the snow as they guided her forward. They passed under the darkened marquee of the Cartier cinema, peeked into the Castel, but moved on when they noticed it was full. They continued east, in the direction of the Four Corners, and stopped in front of Mexi-Go.

❧

Neither Willy Eyamie, owner of the Castel, nor José Flores, owner of Mexi-Go, paid much attention to the people outside their restaurants between three and four on Saturday and Sunday mornings. Even in these early hours of New Year's Day, when altercations and other incidents escalated in frequency, rarely did one offer enough novelty to draw the staff's attention away from the regular turnover of customers if they kept their focus indoors. Consequently, the attention of the two proprietors—both on duty that morning—was not drawn to the commotion out front. Nor was Flores able later to recall seeing a group consisting of two native women—one physically supporting the other—and three twentyish white men enter his restaurant. This particular group of customers was no more notable for its blend of ethnicities and states of mind than the group that had just left. On the strip, people mingled indiscriminately at this time of the morning.

David and Joyce kept Minnie standing as the five of them pushed their way into Mexi-Go. With Michel leading the way, they maintained an alternately plodding and urgent pace past the cash register at the front of the restaurant, then along what seemed to be an endless row of stools that lined the counter. Finally, they reached a point where the room opened up to a dozen or so old wooden tables surrounded by too many chairs, half of them missing rungs from their backs. Patrick looked for an empty table. Along the back wall he spotted one that had yet to be cleared; he signalled the waitress to hold it for them.

The table had only four chairs around it, so Patrick grabbed a fifth one from a nearby table. But instead of sitting, he knelt in front of Minnie while Joyce and David lowered her into one of the chairs. Michel didn't sit either; he stayed clear of the table altogether, still upset and trying to collect himself. Standing over by the counter, he surveyed the restaurant then returned his attention to Minnie. *If he hadn't known what had happened, he would have thought Minnie looked like any other drunk in the room.*

He shook his head over and over again while Patrick held Minnie's hand and persistently asked how she was doing. Minnie responded, not with words, but with an incoherent, "Er-r-r-r-r, er-r-r-r-r, er-r-r-r-r."

When the waitress finally came over to clear the table, David ordered coffee, but only for Joyce and Minnie.

Coroner's Inquest Testimony – Patrick Smith

A. ...And we sat Minnie down there and we talked to
her, and she seemed to be getting a little more
coherent...she certainly wasn't able to articulate
anything with–you know...to a fluent degree or anything, but...after a few attempts, Dave was able to
get her number from her, and I think an attempt at
her address as well, and we got Joyce's number
and–and address, and then we said–like, we talked
with them for a little while, it was pretty crowded
and we talked with them for a little while and we
said, you know, to Joyce "Make sure you do get her
an ambulance."

Michel, David, and Patrick were experiencing an uneasy calm.
They said little to one another, but the few words they uttered
echoed the responsibility they felt to make a crucial life-or-death-
type decision. Each one grappled with his inability to make the
situation disappear. David had tried to call for help, but it wasn't
his fault that Hull didn't have 911 service. Michel had attempted
to move the police officers to duty, but had only succeeded in making them angrier, and, in the process, making a fool of himself.
And Patrick, who had maintained his composure throughout the
ordeal, was plagued by an uncanny feeling that this dismal situation wasn't over; it had just moved indoors. They all agreed on one
thing, though: *Minnie did look better now that she was out of the cold
and sitting in a chair with a cup of coffee in front of her.*

Coroner's Inquest Testimony – Michel Filion

Q. All right, but at the restaurant, there was no further
attempts made to call an ambulance when you got in
there.

A. There wasn't no further attempt for us, because

after what we saw from the cops, they—what they did to her, then we said, "Oh, my gosh," then she must be all right, or something like that, and then we were—I was so shock (sic) from what happened, and I thought policemen were there to protect us, first of all, and—and when you ask a policeman to call an ambulance, I thought they had to call an ambulance, if you asked them.

Q. O.K. All right. But, again, to be fair to everyone, you didn't call an ambulance, either...

A. No, I didn't.

The boys discussed once again what they should do and this time agreed that Minnie was probably more shaken by the accident than physically hurt. Her expression was less confused and, while she didn't respond, her face would turn and stay focused on whoever was speaking at the time. She also didn't show any visible signs of physical injury, and even managed to utter a few sounds.

Sensing that Minnie would, somehow, be okay, but wanting to put some closure to what had happened, Patrick made a passing comment about Minnie and Joyce suing the Hull police. Minnie responded with another "Er-r-r-r," followed by a few murmurs that sounded like "Forget about money." Before he got up from kneeling in front of Minnie, Patrick read aloud the telephone number Joyce had given him and assured her that one of them would call to inquire how Minnie was doing.

Coroner's Inquest—Cross-Examination – Michel Filion

A. ...when we left, we said to Joyce, "Are you going to call an ambulance, Joyce?" and she said, "Yeah." Then I said we'll leave it to Joyce, so we—it's her friend and she'll take care of her. That's what she said. "She's my cousin; I'll take care of her" and then that's when she decide to leave—or we leave.

The three students had barely been in the restaurant for ten minutes, but when the crisp morning air washed over them, it seemed as if they had been cooped up inside the smoky grill for hours. The past half hour was a blur. One minute they were congratulating themselves for going to Hull when they could have just as easily gone to bed; the next they were quickly sobering up in the face of a bewildering incident.

It was after four a.m., and they had no trouble getting a cab. All the way home, they talked about what had happened, rehashing their indignation over the police officers' actions, and convincing one another that Minnie hadn't been seriously hurt.

Back at the apartment, they continued talking for a good two hours. Before they finally went to bed, Patrick assured his friends that he would call Joyce.

Coroner's Inquest Testimony – Joyce Wesley

A. ...I told Minnie, "I'll call an ambulance" and she told me she was all right, and I didn't know what to do after that when she told me she was all right. And she told me that she–she–she needs to go to the bathroom to go throw up, so I helped her to the bathroom, and I told her, Minnie, I'll wait for you outside, because, when I look at her throw up, I want to throw up myself, so she said O.K. So I went back down to my seat and waited for her and she came up–she came out and I met her halfways and helped her sit back down on her seat, and I kept asking her if she was all right and she said yes.

Not everyone in Mexi-Go was oblivious to the group that occupied the table next to the washrooms. Three Somali men sitting at a nearby table were watching Joyce's every move with great interest. Twenty-two-year-old Abdi Ibrahim, a recent immigrant, and his two friends, Mohammed and Abraham, had experienced no luck meeting women that night at Zinc, a dance bar just down the strip from J.R.'s. They left Zinc before last call so that they could get a table at the Castel, but skipped over to Mexi-Go when they found it full.

The three men had arrived at Mexi-Go just minutes before Minnie, Joyce, and the boys. They had watched with amusement while Minnie and Joyce slumped down at the table as if dumped by a luggage trolley. Their eyes had been firmly fixed on Joyce–the tall one–from the moment she came in, first on her long black hair as it bounced with each stride, then on the movements of her large form as she tried to sober up her friend.

Joyce could sense their interest, but was used to such attention and wasn't interested this morning in returning glances or being flattered by anyone's offer of a drink or anything else. Not at the moment, anyway. She had enough on her mind with Minnie, who was barely managing to sit up straight and who looked ready to doze off any second.

Coroner's Inquest Testimony – Abdi Ibrahim

Q. Now, could you tell us how it happened that you and your friends met these two women in the restaurant in Hull?

A. Actually, when we came from the club, we straight went to the restaurant, to at least have couple of drinks. So there was the place that we met them, actually.

Q. O.K. And how come you started speaking to them?

A. You see, actually, I was not the one who have start asking them to give them a ride. The other two guys who were with me, one of them asked them to–if he can give them a ride to the place where they are living...

Abdi's friend, Mohammed, was first to come over. In order to start a conversation with Joyce, he faked interest in the well-being of the person slumped in the chair next to her. So intent was he on his come-on, he was unable to recognize that Joyce was not remotely interested in him.

Why doesn't he just go away, Joyce thought, trying her best to act sober and keep Minnie from falling to the floor, which would cause them both to be thrown out by the proprietor.

Suddenly, Minnie mumbled that she had to throw up again. Seeing Joyce rise to escort her, Mohammed returned to his table. Once Minnie was positioned over the toilet, Joyce came out and paced nervously at the washroom door.

Coroner's Inquest Testimony – Joyce Wesley

A. And I got up and when I saw the door—the washroom door opening, she came out and she almost fell, but I caught her, and I helped her back to her seat. And when we got back to our seat, another black guy came—came there. He was wearing a black tweed coat and he was trying to pick us up, like, he came over, bending down, saying—he told me that I could give you anything you want, and I was just looking at him and he says, "Why don't we go over to my place and go have a couple of beers and your friend can sleep it off at my place?"

Joyce was tired of unwanted advances from strangers. Under different circumstances she might have accepted a drink or engaged in some casual conversation, but now her thoughts were focused on what she should do with Minnie. It was too late to call her husband, Billy, to come and pick them up—the kids couldn't be left alone—and she didn't have enough money for a cab. Even if Billy could come she didn't even know where Minnie lived. *Somewhere near Scott Street*, she vaguely recalled.

She regretted not having had the presence of mind to tag

along with the boys when they left. Without them there, she felt isolated and helpless, uncertain of what might happen to them next. The night had taken on the aura of a lame circus—how could she and Minnie be expected to walk a tightrope when they couldn't follow a straight line? The evening was supposed to be fun, and that was it. Instead, it had turned serious, and their fate was far less certain than it had been when she and Minnie set out with Sam just hours before.

The man in the black tweed coat who had tried to pick Joyce up minutes before wandered over again. Just then, Mohammed's young friend, Abdi, jumped up from their nearby table.

- -

Police Statement – *Joyce Wesley*
(actual written statement)

Minnie, I was going to call an ambulance and she
said she was ok that's all she said. I kept asking
her, "that right, are you ok" and she kept saying
"I'm alright." One black guy tried to pick us up
and that's when Abdi said stay away he is bad
news. Minnie had already gwent to the bathroom
twice to throw up before Abdi spoke to us.
and offered to drive us home and I told
him could I trust you says he said yes, and I
told him everybody says yes but I didn't trust him
but he said we don't hurt women and I said ok
lets go.
They helped me with Minnie, and we put her
in the front seat with the seat belt on and we
asked her for her address and she said Laurier

The group that rose to leave Mexi-Go was different from the one that had arrived a half hour before. On the way in, Joyce and Minnie were flanked by three young men who appeared not only to know them, but also to be intimately involved with their condition and genuinely concerned for their well-being. The three men who led them out barely spoke to them. The group's exit had an air of finality, victors leading their victims. Only Joyce didn't feel like a victim; she felt like someone who was simply relieved to have someone take over for a little while.

On the way out, Joyce told Minnie in Cree that they were going home to sleep it off. She added that these men had promised not to hurt them and that *everything will turn out all right*.

The car, which was parked in a small commercial lot around the corner from the restaurant, belonged to Mohammed. But it was Abdi who issued directions to everyone, including how to get to the vehicle. Abdi suggested that he, Joyce, and Abraham sit in the back so that Minnie could have more legroom in the front. Together, the three of them folded Minnie into the front seat while Mohammed scraped ice from the front and back windows.

Just as Mohammed took the driver's seat, Minnie's head fell toward the dashboard. He pushed her back into position and pulled the seat belt across her shoulder, snapping it tight before starting the engine.

Coroner's Inquest–Cross-Examination – Joyce Wesley

Q. In any event, from what you've told us, she told you on more than one occasion that she was all right.

A. Yes.

Q. And you asked her specifically whether she wanted you to call an ambulance?

A. I beg your pardon?

Q. Did you ask her specifically?

A. Did I ask her?

Q. Whether she wanted you to call an ambulance?

A. No. I told her I'll call an ambulance, but she told me she was all right.

Chapter Seven

NIGHTCAP

You get it the most when you get into a cab. You say Lowrey and they have no idea where it is.... A lot of people pronounce it Laurie, as in the name, which is really confusing because it sounds more like Laurier, which is another street.
— MICHAEL BELLEFEUILLE
Tenant, 18 Lowrey Street

Portage Bridge seamlessly crosses the Ottawa River, joining the two cities of Hull and Ottawa as if they were one. By day, cars crawl bumper-to-bumper in both directions along its six divided lanes to reach government offices on either side of the river. In the evening–especially on weekends–the lanes heading north, toward Hull, hum with the anticipation of joy seekers.

A mile upstream, at one of the river's lowest points, the rusting Chaudière Bridge steals under the roofs of the oldest part of the E. B. Eddy paper plant, past the falls that explain the paper industry's presence in this particular place, and across the shallows into Ottawa's Lebreton Flats. Unlike the Portage Bridge, which escorts its patrons to the most elegant part of Ottawa, the Chaudière dumps its travellers into a vast field. Once a community for thousands of mill hands, the field separates the capital's regal buildings from the rundown townhouses and dilapidated tenements typical of the Flats and nearby Mechanicsville.

Abdi Ibrahim and his friends chauffeured Minnie and Joyce across the Portage Bridge–not the Chaudière–and cruised into the domain of the Parliament Buildings–not the tangled backstreets of the ghetto farther west. In the car, Minnie sat next to Mohammed. Her body was held upright by the shoulder belt; her head lolled back and forth from its resting position on her chest. Except for the random sounds that bubbled through her nostrils, Minnie said nothing the whole way. Occasionally, her breathing paused; eventually she would exhale, releasing the stink of malt and prompting an expletive from someone in the car.

In the back seat, Joyce sat between Abdi and Abraham. The quiet realization that they were travelling in the wrong direction settled in Joyce's mind as she observed the majestic buildings of Parliament Hill passing on her left. She hoped that, somehow, Mohammed would know where to turn and that they would ultimately reach Minnie's home. She wished she could tell him where it was, or even describe what the place looked like, but all she knew was that it sounded like Laurie Street. It wasn't until they churned through the snow past Confederation Square, crossed the Rideau Locks, and skipped over to Sandy Hill that Joyce spoke up and insisted that *Minnie doesn't live down here.*

Coroner's Inquest Testimony – Abdi Ibrahim

Q. Now, do you know what address you were looking for?

A. Yeah. Her friend told us that she's live on Laurier East, but she didn't tell us about the address and all this.

Q. And was it Laurier or Laurie?

A. Laurier East.

Q. That's what you were looking for.

A. Yeah.

Despite her towering presence in places like the Claude Tavern and J. R. Dallas, Joyce felt out of place in Sandy Hill, especially on Laurier Avenue East, a street that paid tribute to Sir Wilfrid Laurier, Canada's prime minister in the late nineteenth century, and one in a long line of men who had betrayed her people. The farther they travelled down Laurier, the more urgently she wanted to get away from that part of town. In fact, the mere sound of the name *Laurier* being bandied about in the car made her want to scream to her companions that *Minnie doesn't live anywhere near here... she lives under the bridge over by Scott Street.*

Coroner's Inquest Testimony – Joyce Wesley

Q. Did you know where she lived?
A. All I know is she lived on Scott Street.
Q. I thought it was Laurie Street or...
A. Yeah, Laurie Street is nearby Scott Street.

The instant recognition bestowed on Laurier Avenue could not be extended to Lowrey, a narrow, block-long road tucked away in the heart of Mechanicsville. While unknown to most people in Ottawa, Lowrey's modest size and the transience of its residents made it one of the best-known streets to Mechanicsville residents.

Had any of the group even heard of Lowrey Street, Minnie would have been home within minutes of their departure from Hull, provided they had crossed the Chaudière Bridge. But by the time Joyce insisted that Minnie did not live on Laurier, she and her companions were lost.

❦

Frustration mounted among the three Somali men as they found themselves in uncharted territory. Like everyone else who had encountered Joyce and Minnie after the accident, they, too, wanted distance from the situation, or at least from Minnie. All of them had seen women drunk before, but this one really couldn't handle her liquor: she looked more unconscious than asleep. As time passed, they found it harder to justify why they didn't just drop both ladies off at the next stop light.

When someone in the car commented that it had stopped snowing, they all agreed that until they decided what to do next, Minnie could use some fresh air. Mohammed pulled off the road into a parking lot near the intersection at Nelson Street, next to the Four Jays restaurant. As he got out of the car, he pulled his seat forward to allow Joyce and Abdi to climb out of the back and help him with Minnie. They circled the automobile from behind to determine the best way to lift out of the car what felt like a sack of potatoes with legs dangling from it.

Together, the three pulled Minnie out, Abraham giving a token push from the back seat. At first they tried to lift her into a standing position, *get her to walk a bit, give her a chance, without coffee and cold water, to sober up.* But Minnie was in no condition to do any walking, even with help. Someone suggested holding her under the arms and pulling her along, which Joyce rejected on the basis that dragging her like the cops in Hull had wouldn't do any good, that they may as well set her on the ground. First, they eased her into a sitting position, then, when she kept falling forward into a heap, they lowered her onto her back.

Mohammed took it upon himself to call 911. He left Abdi and Joyce with Minnie and signalled to Abraham, still in the car, that he was going to the pay phone in front of the restaurant. After making the call, his feeling of helplessness gave way to an overwhelming sense of relief, shared, moments later, by the others. None of them, especially Joyce, were too thrilled with having to deal with the police, but surely the call would produce someone who would get Minnie home.

Ottawa Police Alert Message, January 1, 1989, 4:46 a.m.

Elderly female outside, corner of Laurier and Nelson. Uncertain what problem is. Sitting on the sidewalk. Ambulance is on the way. 10-25 (sick or injured person).

Sabrina Corneanu picked up the call in her cruiser, a few minutes drive from where Minnie lay. She had been a police officer on the Ottawa force for seven years, working first in communications, then court security, on the information desk for a while, and, since last September, on patrol. For New Year's Eve, she had been assigned to car 312-C with the plum assignment of patrolling Sandy Hill, one of the better districts, particularly when the many students who populated the area were on holidays out of town. Because of the small likelihood of trouble erupting in Sandy Hill, even on the biggest drinking night of the year, she was alone in her car.

As she approached the parking lot next to the Four Jays, she spotted a tall woman waving her down from the middle of the road. At first, she anticipated a situation like any of the other calls she had already responded to that night: someone was flat out drunk and unco-operative; someone had been punched out in the parking lot; or maybe the woman staggering over to her car with arms flailing about was a neighbourhood resident who had been pushed around by a husband or boyfriend who was equally drunk.

Ottawa Police Statement – *Joyce Wesley*
(actual written statement)

number and at that time Minnie's legs went weak
and we put her down on the sidewalk, on her rear
end, and then we lay her down on her back. We
waited for the ambulance. I don't know how long
we waited. When we waited for the ambulance I
was with Minnie thats when I saw that police car
coming towards us. Before the female cop could
park her car I was on the road, trying to flag her
down. She said just a minute I'll park to the side.
She did that, she came out, she asked me what
happened. I told her my friend got hit and I don't
know if she is drunk or shes
hurt. She asked me if I could take her home. I
told her no because there wasn't no cops. I told
her I could not leave her here, she might freeze. She
said ok I'll take her in. I don't know if anyone
heard me say that to her, you have to go ask them
yourself. I don't recall if anyone checked Minnie but
I think the female cop did   she asked me whats your

SIGNATURE: _____

Joyce Wesley
Brian Schaaf

friends name →

> and I said Minnie, I think the female cup said
> Minnie are you alright. The big fat guy the
> ambulance driver was there and that's all I
> remember. I don't remember anything more because
> I was heavily intoxicated. Even though I am heavily
> intoxicated I remember some of the things and some
> of the things I don't remem ember. I don't remember
> how I got home, oh no I got a taxi home. I took a
> Taxi home from Lees Ave. I went up to Abdi's
> apartment 190 Lees Apt 1804 and he called me a taxi
> from there. There was a single bed in the

Joyce *was* intoxicated and on closer inspection, it appeared that the woman lying on the ground next to the late-model car was, too.

Constable Corneanu got down as close as she could to Minnie's face to see if she was breathing, then recoiled quickly at the unmistakable odour of beer and vomit. She asked Joyce for her friend's name and was told that the woman was her cousin and that her name was Minnie. Abdi and Mohammed drifted toward their car.

Coroner's Inquest Testimony – Constable Sabrina Corneanu

Q. Did you obtain an account as to what had happened?

A. Yes, I asked a cousin, and she said she [Minnie] had been drinking...

Q. ...Yes, what else happened?

A. I tried to wake her up.

Q. How did you do that?

A. I called her name. I shook her. I didn't get any response.

Constable Corneanu could not rouse Minnie to consciousness. Just then, an ambulance pulled up next to them in the parking lot. Two attendants got out of the ambulance and walked over to where Joyce was speaking with Constable Corneanu. The driver, a big man named Brian Moloughney, asked what was going on while his partner, Donna Parker, stood by, waiting. Constable Corneanu said that she presumed the lady was drunk. Moloughney asked for her name and was told it was Minnie.

Coroner's Inquest Testimony – Brian Moloughney

A. I–I attempted to extract more information from the bystanders present. I asked, "Could you tell me what had happened?" and again, the lady that was talking to the officer told us that they had come from a house on Nelson Street, she pointed in a south direction, they were walking towards Laurier Street when the lady had fallen down.

Coroner's Inquest–Cross-Examination – Joyce Wesley

Q. Did you talk to the ambulance attendant at all?

A. No. All I know is that I saw the ambulance attendant talking to the female cop, but I don't know what they were saying.

Moloughney went over to where Minnie lay alone next to the car. He said "hello" loudly, then, when she didn't respond, proceeded to give her a sternal rub, which by applying pressure to her breastbone with his fist would surely cause pain and illicit a response. Joyce kept an eye on the brief examination, all senses tuned to Minnie, anxious for a groan, a movement of her head, or a call for her glasses, which she remembered picking up from the slush on rue Principale in Hull and placing over Minnie's eyes. But Minnie's body remained still.

When Moloughney checked Minnie's pupils, Joyce half expected him to comment that she was blind, that her left eye was completely white, but he didn't say anything about her eyes. He just got up and wandered back to where the others huddled by the police car. He confirmed what the police officer had suspected: Minnie was drunk.

Coroner's Inquest Testimony – Brian Moloughney

Q. And how, according to the police officer, she's totally unresponsive, passed out, doesn't say a word all along...unconscious, and according to [you], she's responsive and is able to say she doesn't feel any pain and is able to decide that she doesn't want to go to the hospital. You're both at the same place at the same time?

A. We're at the same place at the same time, but she did her pressure point check prior to my arrival.

Q. Um-hmm.

A. And I'm telling you what my findings were.

Moloughney suggested that Constable Corneanu take Minnie in her cruiser to the detoxification unit so that she could dry up. The officer agreed and went to call the dispatcher, who verified that the detoxification unit on nearby Bruyère Street had a bed.

In an attempt to get her to walk, the two ambulance attendants and the police officer proceeded to pull Minnie into a sitting, then a standing, position. When Minnie's body showed no signs of co-operating, Moloughney and Parker scooped her up and deposited her in the back of the cruiser.

As the police cruiser pulled away, Joyce and her companions piled back into Mohammed's car and left.

Ambulance attendants Moloughney and Parker also returned to their vehicle and left. According to the Ottawa-Carleton Regional

Ambulance Service Incident and Occurrence Report for January 1, 1989, only five minutes had passed since their arrival at, and departure from, the scene.

Coroner's Inquest Testimony – Brian Moloughney

Q. Is this the report that you're referring to here?

A. That's correct.

Q. O.K. Is there a name of a patient there?

A. No, I don't have a name.

Chapter Eight
LOWER TOWN LULLABY

*As far as we're concerned, we did what
we were supposed to, what was our
mandate. And that was in our best
interest, because, had we taken her, she
would have died without medical
attention on one of our cots.*
— CARL HUDON
Sisters of Charity
Detoxification Centre

New Year's Eve wasn't busier than any other night at the Sisters of
Charity Detoxification Centre in Ottawa's Byward Market. The
clients served by the centre were seasoned alcoholics: boozers with
a passion for liquor whether they were on their way to a party or at
home watching television. Such drinkers didn't consume more alcohol because it was New Year's Eve; they drank as much on New
Year's Eve as they had the night before, and the night before that.

When the call from the police dispatcher came in, Marie
Louise Boudreau, the centre's supervisor, put the caller on hold
while she checked the files. She wanted to see whether someone
by the name of Minnie had ever been admitted before, and, if so,
whether she had caused a disturbance and had to be referred elsewhere. When she discovered that no one by that name had been
registered in the centre's log over the past few months, she told the
dispatcher to send the woman along; they had a couple of extra
beds and one would be ready for her.

Marie Louise pondered the characteristics of this guest. Old?
Young? Lethargic and about to pass out? Violent and ready to

fight? *Most likely some harmless soul who wandered off from her friends.* That she had been referred by the police was nothing unusual; "Minnie" was only one of many that the police referred to the centre each week.

After setting the receiver down, she checked the clock: it was almost time for the resident check required every half hour. At four-thirty, seventeen of the nineteen guests had been asleep. Judging by the silence upstairs, the remaining two were out as well.

She had no sooner started the rounds when the bell sounded from the back of the house. While it seemed she had just gotten the call, she knew it would be the new woman the police had called about.

She asked her colleague, Doris, to continue the resident check while she registered the new guest, then told Carl, the attendant, to get the bed ready.

When she opened the door, Marie Louise found only one person on the step: a female police officer whom she had not met before. Over the officer's shoulder she could see the police cruiser a few feet away, in the narrow lane that cut between the centre's back step and the wall of another old building. Its headlights were on, lighting up the entire lane, and the engine was still running. Both rear doors were open wide; inside she could see a motionless figure stretched out across the rear seat, her head resting on a folded blanket.

Constable Corneanu motioned to the car, saying that she would need help getting the woman in, because she couldn't walk. Marie Louise explained that if the client couldn't walk, the centre couldn't accept her. "We can help her walk in, but she has to walk in."

- -

Ottawa Police Statement –
Marie Louise Boudreau, Supervisor,
Detoxification Centre
At this point, Carl Hudon, Detox attendant, joined me at the door. I then went outside and tried to wake her

up–but to no avail. I explained to the police officer the detox policy regarding the admission of non-ambulatory persons in the unit. The police officer became quite angry stating that the Detox was not fulfilling its mandate and that he [sic] would put in a complaint against me and the Detox.

The two women got into an uneasy deliberation about the situation. Constable Corneanu insisted that she was unaware of any such policy, and that if there was one, why hadn't the dispatcher been told before she had driven all the way over. Marie Louise pointed out that she must have been in the area anyway, because the call had just come in, and that the police should know the centre's policy by now, having run into the same problem dozens of times before. She also expressed her indignation over the fact that Minnie's condition had not been described to her over the phone; the centre didn't like to turn people away at the door, especially those in Minnie's condition.

Detoxification Centre - Departmental Manual
A MAN/WOMAN WHO IS BROUGHT TO THE CENTRE UNCONSCIOUS AND IMMOBILIZED IS NEVER ADMITTED AT THAT POINT.
If an unconscious man/woman is referred by telephone, the staff instructs the referral individual or agency to convey him/her to the nearest hospital.

Marie Louise noticed immediately that Minnie was native, and also that she looked like many of the centre's regulars: fiftyish, clothed in worn blue jeans and an oversize coat that displayed the markings of many uses and even more falls. She had thick hands marked with calluses and scars. Her fingers were short and stubby, each one crowned with a swatch of ruby-red nail polish. Her complexion was ruddy and spotty all at once—her skin appeared to have been exposed to cold greater than what this night had to offer. Actually, the only outstanding characteristic about the woman was that she wasn't moving.

Marie Louise tried to wake Minnie up by calling her name a few times, quietly at first, then progressively louder. This elicited no response, not even a flinch. She then wiggled Minnie's feet in an attempt to provoke some movement, but felt them both drop back to their flaccid state. She watched the police officer make her way to the other side of the car, then suggested that she take Minnie to the hospital or the police station. In a final attempt to gain a response, Constable Corneanu held Minnie under the chin and gently shook her head. Nothing.

Coroner's Inquest–Cross-Examination –
Marie Louise Boudreau

Q. ...You said that, when you went out to check Minnie in the back seat of the police cruiser...both doors were open. You were at one end; the police officer was at the other end.

A. Um-hmm.

Q. And no response. You told the police officer you couldn't take her and then they left.

A. That's right.

Q. O.K. So you actually did come out of the building.

A. Yeah.

Coroner's Inquest Testimony – Sabrina Corneanu

Q. Did somebody from the detox centre come out and look in your cruiser...

A. No.

Once again this morning, the dilemma of what to do with Minnie Sutherland was left with Sabrina Corneanu. First, an ambulance had been called, and the attendant had said that Minnie was drunk. *No kidding*. Minnie's friend had said that they had been drinking in Hull, and she hadn't seemed too worried. Not enough to hang around, anyway. Now a detoxification centre's staff figured that Minnie was too drunk to stay at their facility, saying that she should be taken to a hospital. Why the hospital? She didn't look sick. Just drunk. DRUNK. Her alternatives for dealing with an incapacitated person whom no one would take off her hands were few—especially when the woman hadn't done anything wrong except get smashed on New Year's Eve like everyone else.

Ottawa Police Statement –
Marie Louise Boudreau, Supervisor, Detoxification Centre
The police officer then proceeded to close the back door of the police car, catching her feet. Before the police officer got in the car, he [sic] demanded to know what he [sic] should do with her (M. Sutherland). We suggested either the hospital or the police station.

After Constable Corneanu left, Marie Louise and Carl went back inside. They heard a sound—someone stirring upstairs—and knew they had better get up there. Experience had taught them that someone simply rolling over in bed could be a prelude to a loud cry or a stream of obscenities that would ignite a chorus of vile commentaries on life and eventually result in vomit being spewed over the staff member trying to calm the guest down. Carl checked the ground floor while Marie Louise raced upstairs. Luckily, Doris already had the man under control before any of the other guests woke up and formed a relay. This time a few soothing words had done the trick, together with a chaser of Tylenol to ease his headache.

Another call came from the police station with a referral. Marie Louise took this call, too. *I hope this one knows the centre's policy*, she thought and asked if the person could stand. While talking, she glanced out the window. She noticed there were almost no cars in the street, uncommon for a road that also housed the city's main palliative care hospital, where visitors came and went at all hours. Then one puttered by with two people close together in the front seat: a couple who had just spent their first New Year's Eve together or, just as easily, members of a family that had just shared its last.

Marie Louise looked at her watch; it was past five o'clock. She went into the office to update the logbook.

Detoxification Centre Log –
January 1, 1989 (actual written excerpt)

> 05 00   Resident check   / up 19 down   D.M.
>
> (05:00   Sutherland, Minnie refused at the door –
> passed out in Police Cruiser – could not walk her
> up.   M.L.)
>
> 05 00   Call back
>
> 05:30   Doug on break + off

Coasting up Parent Street toward the Byward Market, Constable Corneanu radioed ahead to the station and told the dispatcher she was coming in. She drove slowly, not quite certain why she was bringing in the woman conked out in the back seat, equally sure that she had to bring her in because no one else would take her.

Had it been a few hours earlier, the market would have been crawling with activity–seasonal cheer served up in fifty odd bistros and cafés in the area, mayhem encouraged in a half-dozen neighbourhood bars with traditions dating as far back as that of the farmer's market for which the area was named. Now the doors of the establishments were secured with bars, the parking lots empty, and deep tracks in the snow were dotted with glass from beer bottles tossed out to salute the New Year as cars sped off.

Driving through the Byward Market at this hour gave people Sabrina Corneanu's age a glimpse of an era they had only heard about. Once, people said, the market was more than a place to have cappuccino and dessert.

Until the 1960s, the market was ablaze with the comings and goings of the working class from up the valley and down, people popping in and out of fish stores, ordering meat by the quarter, and lugging sacks from dry goods stores nestled next to one another behind vegetable stalls.

Back then, they would say, the market was "no place to go at night," save for "bums" chewing at the remnants from the vegetable crates emptied at the end of each day, and "ladies of the night" leaning against the poles that, during the day, secured the canvas drapes of the farmers' stalls.

It was still no place to go in the early hours of the morning. Near the intersection at George and Dalhousie, a man in a torn overcoat sat crouched on the sidewalk; one hand cradled a plastic bag overflowing with assorted bits of garbage, an empty container of rubbing alcohol lay next to him. A tall black girl in a short skirt and open waistcoat crossed the road. Oblivious to the man at the corner and to any vehicles waiting to turn, she marched across the road proudly, her stare set somewhere far in the distance, her hands rubbing her arms to keep warm.

❧

Constable Corneanu pulled into the underground sally-port at the Ottawa police headquarters at 5:12 a.m. She had already radioed ahead and warned them about Minnie and her condition. The dispatcher told her that Sergeant Givogue, who was in charge of the cell block that night, would be waiting for her.

Ottawa Police Statement –
Sergeant Luc Givogue
This officer will indicate that he was in charge of the cell block area on Jan. 1, 1989 and that he did examine a female person now identified as Minnie Sutherland who was laying [sic] in the back seat of Cst. Corneanu's police vehicle in the sally-port area of the Ottawa police station.

Outside her cruiser, Constable Corneanu repeated to Sergeant Givogue what had happened: she had been summoned to a Priority 2 call on Laurier East and found a woman lying on the ground in the parking lot next to the Four Jays restaurant, obviously drunk and accompanied by another lady who was drunk as well. The ambulance arrived shortly after she had and one of the attendants examined the woman and agreed that she was drunk. She then recounted her experience at the detoxification centre and expressed her bewilderment about what she was expected to have done after such a reception.

Sergeant Givogue peered into the back seat of the cruiser to get a better look at Minnie. To his eyes, she appeared unconscious. The smell in the car confirmed for him, too, that she was drunk. He looked at her head to see if injuries from a fall or a fight were evident. In an attempt to get some sort of physical response, he applied pressure under Minnie's nose, then under her chin and ears. Her head moved, maybe an inch, but that was all. Her facial expression didn't change, her eyes stayed shut, and the rest of her body remained motionless.

Coroner's Inquest Testimony – Sergeant Luc Givogue

Q. Now, the ambulance attendants saw her at around five o'clock in the morning, a few minutes earlier, and placed her in the police car and yet, they have testified, or at least one has testified that she in fact was able to speak and indicate she didn't want to go to the hospital and wanted to go to the detox centre. Did she appear to you in any way to be a person in that type of condition who could speak and communicate?

A. When she was brought to the sally-port, no, definitely not.

Contrary to Ottawa Police Department policy, which did not allow officers to convey anyone to hospital by car, unless the person was a prisoner, Sergeant Givogue ordered Constable Corneanu to take Minnie to the hospital in her cruiser. He wasn't satisfied that the ambulance attendants had done their job properly, either, but he wasn't about to call and have it out with them over the phone. And it didn't seem right to book the unconscious woman when she hadn't done anything wrong. Besides, Minnie's level of unconsciousness appeared to be far too deep for any other course of action.

As Constable Corneanu got ready to leave, Sergeant Givogue insisted, "Get her checked, and I don't care what arguments you have to use, get her checked by a doctor. If he's satisfied, or if he will not admit her, then bring her back, and I will have no choice but to lodge her in the cells."

At 5:45 a.m., Minnie was helped out of Constable Corneanu's cruiser by emergency room staff at the Ottawa General Hospital. The triage nurse found Minnie's full name by rummaging through her purse, which had somehow remained with her throughout the ordeal. The only other history she obtained was from Constable Corneanu, who claimed that Minnie was found on the street, apparently drunk.

As she left the hospital, Sabrina Corneanu updated her duty book.

Minnie Sutherland.
Dr. Peacock.
Admitted at General Hospital.
Found on Laurier and Nelson.

ॐ

Dr. Margaret Peacock, the doctor on duty that morning, took several blood samples and inspected Minnie for injuries that might have caused her state of unconsciousness. She noted that while Minnie's vital signs were stable, she was hypothermic. Although not a good state, hypothermia was not unusual in someone discovered on the streets in winter. The smell of alcohol was also evident on Minnie's breath.

A couple of hours passed and Dr. Peacock was still unable to rouse Minnie. She discussed her patient's condition with the doctor taking over Emergency for the next shift; they agreed she should be admitted for further examination.

Ottawa Police Department
Regulations and Procedures Manual
CARE OF PERSONS IN CUSTODY
When on duty, a duty N.C.O. shall: ensure the safekeeping of all persons in custody and should any become unconscious or appear to be in acute distress from illness or injury, intoxication or reaction from any drug, have him/her taken to the nearest hospital, ensuring that all established policies and procedures respecting the handling of the person in custody are adhered to.

...The particulars of a person taken to hospital as a result of compliance with this section shall be obtained and an Occurrence Report submitted.

Constable Corneanu did not complete an Occurrence Report until twelve days later. By then, interest in Minnie Sutherland was intense. Suddenly, the woman who Hull police called "squaw" and who Ottawa police didn't know what to do with, was a public figure, her death seen as an unfortunate consequence of inaction, prejudice, and neglect. But despite the fact that she had become a household name in Ottawa, and a single photograph of her had been recycled among dozens of newspapers nationally, nobody really knew who Minnie Sutherland was.

Part Three
THE STARS

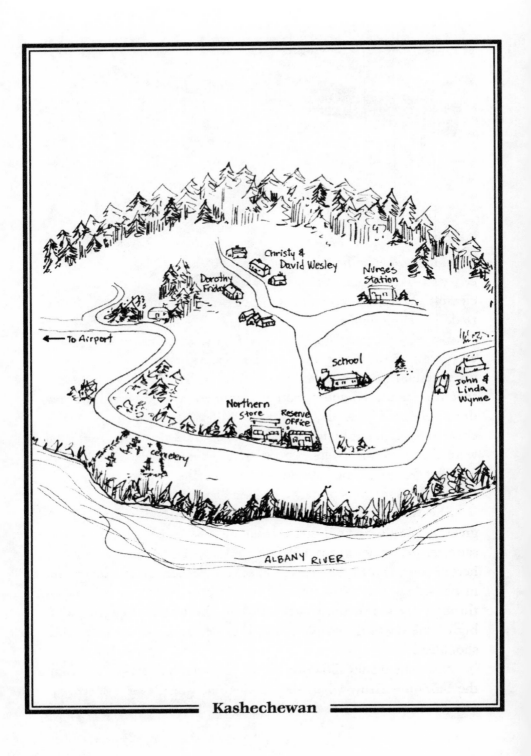

Kashechewan

Chapter Nine

FIVE A.M. SHARP

She never wanted a husband but she
loved kids.

— DOREEN MILBURY

Teaching someone how to smoke was no easy task. Not for eighteen-year-old Minnie Sutherland, who treated the act of smoking a cigarette as a social art—something to practise alone if you wanted to do it well in public.

For Minnie, practising her cigarette smoking was not an isolated performance. Along with it came the right clothes and make-up, a certain posture, sultry moves, and an attitude. She believed that you should be appropriately costumed, as you would for the dress rehearsal of a play, and make a dry run without an audience—except, possibly, for a friend who could tell you what you were doing wrong. A cigarette within her own walls always gave Minnie the confidence she needed to take herself on the road to one of the nightclubs or dance halls she favoured.

She would usually wear something nice: one of her bright green or purple cocktail dresses that, because of her height, trailed satin far below her knees. (If it was summer and she was readying herself for a trip to the beach, she would prance around the room in her bikini, posing in front of each mirror for hours and going through a good dozen smokes.) Then she would tease her hair high, glue on long red nails, and dab perfume on her neck and shoulders.

Next, she would slide over to the hi-fi she had picked up from the Salvation Army when she first moved to Ottawa and set the one 45 she owned on the turntable: "A Single Girl" by Sandy

Posey. It was her absolute favourite; a song that seemed to justify her move from the family home in Moose Factory to Ottawa. The song always put her in the right mood.

Dipping and sliding her way across the room, Minnie would flip the switch of the table lamp as she passed it, pull the overhead string to cut the direct light, and pick up the brass lighter that an old boyfriend had given her. With a flick of her thumb, she would throw the cap open, then adjust the fuel feed to make sure the flame would flare as high as she wanted it to.

A lit Rothmans between her fingers, she would ease into the recliner, cross her legs and let the rising hemline reveal one knee, then the other. Recline, but not all the way. With the first puff, she'd let her head fall back seductively, inhale and purse her lips, letting the smoke flow out like a stream of cool mist.

ℬ

Maggie Bugden, Minnie's best friend in those days, tried time and time again to achieve such grace, but she never could. Minnie told her it was because she was, at nineteen, too old to learn new tricks. Maggie knew it was because she got more pleasure out of watching Minnie do it than in trying to do it herself.

ℬ

Minnie and Maggie met in Ottawa in 1966 while attending a government-sponsored adult education program to complete high school. They came from opposite shores of James Bay, but had friends in common, mostly from towns such as Timmins and North Bay, which were popular native communities long before the government sponsored the establishment of reserves on both sides of the bay.

Already in the program for a year, Minnie was settled in both school and social life. She had a number of budding friendships, both native and white, and lots of acquaintances. She knew where to get the cheapest bottle of Coke in Vanier, and where on the train line the carnival vans parked to unload their rides and show tents for the fair each summer. She knew where all the movie theatres were, could show you where Elvis Presley played a concert before he became famous, and could point you in the direction of the Diamond Barbecue on Bank Street, where they served the best "Chicken on a Bun" in town.

Minnie's roommate, another James Bay Cree named Beatrice Jonah, was also attending the school; so was Minnie's first native acquaintance in Ottawa, Evelyn Mark. Shortly after Maggie arrived, Evelyn finished the program and started looking for a job. Evelyn's absence in the school's halls between classes, and in the cafeteria at lunch, allowed Minnie to devote more time to Maggie. The attention served Maggie well; within weeks she felt like an old hand at the school, even giving directions and advice to students who had started at the same time she did.

The hours the two girls spent together were rewarding, especially for Maggie, who found herself getting close to this confident, slightly younger girl with what appeared to be a lifetime of happy experiences under her belt—the kinds of experiences that had eluded her own troubled life back in Fort George, Quebec. She especially liked the way Minnie carried herself—proud, self-assured, dignified—a role model in a world Maggie found not only new, but, at times, intimidating.

Within months, Minnie and Maggie had become best friends, spending most of their free time together. Because the private home in Vanier where Maggie boarded was only a few blocks from the place where Minnie and Beatrice roomed, they also took the bus together, sometimes stopping for a soda after school before going to their separate homes. When Beatrice made a hasty decision to quit the program and leave for her home up north, Minnie asked if there was an available room at the rooming house where Maggie lived. Within a week, they were living together.

Like most young natives new to a city, Minnie and Maggie approached whites with a combination of trust and reticence. On the one hand, they were anxious to meet new people, and let the innocence that had been nurtured by growing up in protective communities give them strength as they explored this environment of concrete and steel. On the other hand, their parents and the elders in their communities had cautioned them about life in the cities. Most of them had been to a big Canadian city at one time or another and had encountered discrimination at almost every turn. Every letter that arrived from Moose Factory or Fort George was filled with warnings about the perils of trusting white people too much, about not forgetting who you are "because they won't," about the dangers of getting caught up with a drinking crowd, and about where you could end up if you were in the wrong place at the wrong time—"then you'll see who you can trust." At first, the barrage of warnings dampened their spirits, but Minnie's enthusiasm was not easily extinguished. And if Maggie started to get depressed, Minnie could snap her out of it in no time, either with a suggestion to go out for a smoke, or a lewd joke that made Maggie blush and forget about home altogether.

Ottawa in 1966 was an exciting place to be. The country was readying itself for a great Centennial celebration that was already drawing international attention. What was most thrilling for Minnie and Maggie was the sudden interest among Canadians in the native heritage of this hundred-year-old country that, in the past, had always aligned itself more with Great Britain or France than with the aboriginal nations that had occupied the land for thousands of years.

Everywhere Minnie and Maggie went in Ottawa, they witnessed transformation. Not the kind they were used to up north, such as an afternoon in the sun watching electricity being strung into the community hospital, or joining a crowd at someone's house as a satellite dish went up.

The change of pace in Ottawa was welcome. Here, Minnie and Maggie could stand for hours in Confederation Square watching the massive National Arts Centre go up. Down the road, they could watch rail lines being ripped up to make way for trees and the smooth, green grass that they saw only in front of white people's houses up north. A few blocks away, they could count the twenty-six storeys of the city's first tower as it climbed into the sky. Then there were movie theatres to go to, Italian and Chinese restaurants, and big grocery stores with shelves full of foods they could only dream of buying before they arrived.

Minnie was an early riser; she had started getting up at five a.m. while working with mentally handicapped children in Waterloo the year before. Maggie wasn't. Try as she might, she always ended up sleeping through the alarm, only to be roused by Minnie's persistent trill about being late for school.

In school, they tried to have lunch together every day; if one had an errand to do, the other willingly tagged along. After school, they would take two buses to get home, taking advantage of the downtown transfer to slip over to Sparks Street and look at the pretty dresses in the windows of the Murphy Gamble department store. In the evening, they would enjoy one of their landlady's hot suppers. To Minnie and Maggie, Mrs. Demers became symbolic of all white people—friendly, hospitable, kind—and they didn't miss an opportunity to tell the folks back home exactly that. Surely the warnings from home that flowed through the postal system every couple of weeks were exaggerations.

Weekend nights, Minnie and Maggie went out. Sometimes they would just go to the "corner" and spend an entire evening in a diner enjoying pop and french fries. Other times, they would call friends and go to a movie or gather at someone's house to watch favourite shows like "I Dream of Jeannie" and "The Brady Bunch." The shared culture of the group intensified their enjoyment of each other's company; they found it comforting to congregate with people who truly related to their background and experiences, and who faced the same challenges in living away from home. The get-togethers were almost always pleasant—until someone started to drink. At that point, the group would dissolve and the fun dissipated as quickly as it had begun.

Every now and then, a few of them, mostly the girls, would go to the Oak Door on Bank Street, where, for a buck cover charge and twenty-five cents a soda, they could spend the whole night listening to a live band covering Beatles and Motown songs and dancing with cute white boys. Minnie enjoyed the Oak Door because she loved to dance; the people who went there had to like to dance, too, because no liquor was served. Maggie liked it because she didn't have to feel guilty about being out with a *drinking crowd*, though most of the crowd would have gladly enjoyed a beer or two if they could have ordered one.

Once every few weeks, on a weekend, they would get together with Evelyn and some of the other Indians living in Vanier, mostly girls a little older than them. Giggling their way into a restaurant, each would order a hamburger and then share a large plate of fries, dousing the order, when it came, with lots of ketchup and vinegar. A good two hours could be spent eating, telling stories, and playing the jukebox. Sometimes they would top off the treat with a couple of milk shakes shared among the group, then huddle outside the restaurant to tell one last joke before saying goodnight.

At these outings, conversations usually centred around what was going on at school—how hard the courses were, how the other students dressed, and how they wished their school was in Vanier so that they wouldn't have to travel all the way across town. The discussion would end up focusing on how nice this teacher was to them or how paranoid that student was when face-to-face with a *real live Indian*. But it was Minnie who would jump to the defence of anyone being criticized. She always gave people who weren't there to defend themselves the benefit of the doubt and maintained that all Indians weren't angels either.

Now and then, one of the boys in their group would suggest going out to a bar, like the Maple Leaf on Montreal Road, the Claude Tavern in Vanier, or the Chaudière in Aylmer. The girls generally tried to quash the idea, though Maggie suspected that Minnie would have gone if she or one of the other girls had agreed to accompany her. On one occasion, one of the boys told Maggie that Minnie and Beatrice used to go with them all the time so why didn't she come too?

It was usually after a lengthy lecture from one of the girls, about the dangers of drinking and squandering all their money on booze, that the girls went home and the boys went out. The next day, at least one of the boys would approach one of them, saying she was right about drinking too much and could he borrow fifty cents until tomorrow. The next week, all was forgotten and he and the others would repeat the same episode.

Sundays were usually spent at home reading or listening to music, or at someone else's place gabbing. In the summer, a bunch of them might take a long afternoon walk along the canal, through downtown, or to Parliament Hill for one of the public festivals or events typical of the nation's capital. After Sunday dinner with Mrs. Demers and the other roomers, they would watch some television, assure one another that they were ready for the week ahead at school—even if they weren't—and write letters to their families back home.

When Minnie was composing a letter home, she would withdraw from her usually focused demeanour and ramble, jumping from topic to topic as her mind wandered. She would be both homesick and glad to be away from home all at once. In one breath, she could insist on how glad she was to be away from her mother then lament about how much she missed her. In one instant she might claim that her father was too calm in the face of adversity then praise him for being able to remain calm when others got out of control.

Invariably, Minnie's talks about home turned into a diatribe about Augustine Scott, an Indian from Fort Albany, Ontario, who was in love with her. Minnie said that she was in love with him, too, but that she was too young to make a commitment and that he should respect her decision to wait.

Talking about being too young to settle down would some-times induce a cigarette mood in Minnie. Maggie, sitting opposite, would revel in the experience and fall over laughing when some-thing didn't proceed as planned, like the time Minnie inadvertent-ly set one of her false fingernails on fire. Then, as suddenly as the smoking mood overtook Minnie, it would disappear. She would start writing another letter, stopping only when she said that her eyes were hurting and that she was going to bed.

❦

Minnie and Maggie lived together for almost a year, studying math, English, and home economics during the day, and learning about each other every evening until they fell asleep laughing. Minnie appreciated Maggie's easygoing nature and told her so. Maggie told Minnie that she was having more fun than she had ever had.

As Christmas approached, both of them started to get excited about trips home for the holidays. They began talking about what they would do when they got home, then found themselves negoti-ating what they would do when they got back. New Year's resolu-tions. Plans for the long Ottawa winter ahead. When they returned, it would be 1967, Centennial year in Canada. They felt privileged to be in the nation's capital during this celebration not to be repeated for another hundred years, and knew that all the kids back home would envy them. They made a pledge to see more movies in the new year, and to get some part-time work so they could make a trip to Expo 67, the World's Fair to be held in Montreal in the spring. Maggie's eyes widened at the prospect until Minnie reasoned that even if they didn't go to Montreal, they could always see the fire-works display on Parliament Hill in July. It was free.

For Maggie, who came to Ottawa plagued by shyness and full of apprehension about meeting new people, the fear of not fitting in had vanished. She had been befriended by possibly the most

wonderful person in the world, someone who wasn't afraid of anything or anyone, especially white people, who, Minnie maintained, had good points too. She looked forward to the experiences that they would share when they returned from their
reserves after the holidays.

They took the same plane as far as Toronto, and hugged each
other as they made their farewells. Maggie watched Minnie's little
legs toddle over to the gate marked *Timmins*, and thought about
how comforting it would be to see those same legs run toward her
in a couple of weeks.

෪

Minnie did not return after the Christmas holidays. A few weeks
later, Mrs. Demers rented out her room to another native girl fresh
from the reserve.

Coroner's Inquest Testimony – Maggie Bugden

A. That's when she left Ottawa, and the next thing I
knew, she was in the hospital in Toronto.

Q. Um-hmm.

A. She was being treated for an eye problem,
you know....

An explanation of Minnie's sudden disappearance came in a
letter sometime in 1967: Minnie was in Toronto undergoing medical tests for her eyes. She had a job sterilizing bottles at the hospital where she was being treated. Her mother was living a couple of
hours away in Kingston and was really depressed because she had a
problem with her eyes, too. Why didn't Maggie come down from
Ottawa to see her?

Maggie did not know that Minnie or any of her family suffered from eye problems. She remembered Minnie complaining

about her eyes hurting now and then, but she'd associated it more with tiredness than a serious medical problem. Maggie realized then that, despite all of Minnie's talk, the girl who opened her heart so easily was really a private person.

Maggie wrote back, and told Minnie how glad she was to hear from her and that she would think about coming to Toronto.

A few letters and many phone calls after that first correspondence, Maggie decided to make the move. Minnie was settled in a new life in Toronto, living in a downtown rooming house with two Hungarian girls. She let Maggie share her room until the landlady, Mrs. Bianco, got to know Maggie and agreed to rent her a room of her own.

Maggie set out to find her own job, gaining confidence from the fact that Minnie had obtained work at Toronto General Hospital. Her search didn't take her far; she found a job as a nurse's aide in the same hospital. Because she and Minnie worked different hours, connecting for lunch or coffee during the day was difficult. Instead, they both looked forward to talking shop when they got home.

In the rooming house, the girls had to manage their own meals. More often than not, they dined out at Fran's or one of the other local restaurants that stayed open twenty-four hours a day and that served an inexpensive, but heaping, plate of food that included soup and rice pudding, one of Minnie's favourite desserts. Other times, they heated up something from a can, a meal that always satisfied their physical hunger, at least. Growing up in isolated communities in the north, both of them had become accustomed to eating canned meats and vegetables. The land around the housing settlements in which they had been raised—mostly dirt, sand, and rocks—was not favourable for growing anything, and hunting and fishing as a means of survival had become part of the past for a lot of Indians.

On weekends, Minnie would cook. She might make a big pot of beef stew, or serve up a mess of spaghetti and meatballs—some-

Minnie's grandparents,
Barbara and Thomas Goodwin

Minnie and father, Bart, 1953

Minnie and mother, Maggie, 1955

Minnie and mother, Maggie, 1955

Maggie Sutherland with children, Minnie and Sidney, 1956

Minnie, age 7

Minnie's first love, Augustine Scott

Minnie working with
handicapped children,
Waterloo, 1966

Minnie in Ottawa, 1967

Maggie Sutherland with daughters, Linda and Minnie, Toronto, 1969

Minnie and daughter, Roseanne, 1969

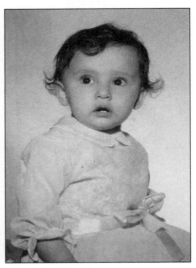

Roseanne, 1970

Violet, age 4

Sisters, Daisy Arthur and
Maggie Sutherland, 1982

Friends Maggie Bugden, Minnie Sutherland,
Evelyn Mark (with Evelyn's son), Ottawa, 1988

Claude Tavern, circa 1980

The Hull Strip, 1989

Linda and John Wynne

Joyce Wesley and husband,
Billy Diamond

Minnie's resting place in Kashechewan

thing that contained her favoured mushrooms and that would last two or three nights and make do for anyone who might drop in and join them.

At least twice they invited native friends, including new friend Mary Hill, for one of Minnie's special bannock breakfasts. As she tossed ingredients into a bowl, she would describe to Maggie and Mary what she was putting into the mix, amusing them with her enthusiasm over something as trivial as blending flour, sugar, egg, milk, and raisins in a bowl. As soon as they started eating, Minnie would pipe up again, chirping between bites about how good her "pancakes" were, and how she knew they were fattening but didn't care.

While Maggie and Minnie routinely reflected on the times they had shared during the previous year in Ottawa, Maggie noticed a number of changes in her friend. The most obvious changes were to her personality; she still had more smiles and kind words to extend in an evening than someone else might have to offer in a month, but she was more cautious about what she said and did. This was most obvious when they went out after work and met others for dinner or coffee. On weekends, it was another matter entirely.

Maggie knew that Minnie had started to drink while living in Waterloo, the year before they first met, but she had never seen Minnie truly drunk in Ottawa. By contrast, it was clear that between the time that Minnie moved to Toronto and when Maggie followed, Minnie and Mary Hill had patronized more than a few bars, and had become regulars in at least one.

Drinking never interfered with Minnie's job, though. Every day she would get up at five a.m. sharp and put in a full day's work, often skipping coffee and lunch breaks. After work, she would head straight home and visit with Maggie and the other girls, entertaining them and having fun until the often agonizing pain in her eyes interfered with her disposition. Then she would excuse herself and retire to her room for the night, where the only sound that carried through the walls would be the erratic burst of snores or the occasional expletive about her eyes.

Minnie reconciled herself to the treatments for her eye problem, but always dreaded the next painful injection that would pierce the lining of each eye and leave her temporarily blind, sometimes for hours. Maggie would always beg off work early that day and escort her friend home in a cab. Throughout the ride, Minnie would cry over the pain and curse her situation, blaming the lack of a regular man in her life on her eyes. Often, she would add something about suicide. When they got to their rooming house, she would go straight to her room and, after taking a couple of pills, drop onto the bed. The next day she'd be up for work again at five.

Come the weekend, Minnie was accountable to no one and nothing, least of all her physical torment. From Friday night to Sunday morning she would party and drink, go out with men who appealed to her, and forget about both her job and the deteriorating condition of her eyes. At these times she ceased to be *Minniesish*–little Minnie–bouncing around Kashechewan with her arms folded tightly around her, and sporting a big smile that upon closer inspection revealed a stranger in this familiar terrain. Now, after putting back a few beers and tucking herself into some man's side, Minnie became the woman she dreamed of being: beautiful, desirable, immune to pain.

A few months later, shortly after Maggie had switched occupations and started working as a clerk for the City of Toronto, Minnie was gone again, this time for over a year. When she reappeared in September 1969, she was seven months pregnant, and accompanied by her mother, Maggie, and her little sister, Linda. Minnie was in town to have an operation for cataracts.

Though excited about having a baby, Minnie appeared sullen, almost defeated. Even once she was settled in a cozy apartment near the hospital, she seemed restless, anxious to leave but determined to stay. After giving birth to a girl, Roseanne, she stayed home for several months. Then she set out to find work, knowing that keeping a steady job would be hard especially with an infant that kept her up half the night. But she knew it was the only way to get on her feet and prove to her mother that she could take care of her new daughter.

Minnie's mother wasn't always convinced by this show of responsibility, and allowed her controlling nature to rule most situations. Though resigned that Minnie had repeated her own mistake of having a child out of wedlock, she was nonetheless disappointed and couldn't help thinking that Minnie would be equally irresponsible in managing other aspects of her life. Such predisposition rarely helped Minnie, who was trying to settle into the trials of motherhood while looking for a decent job. Finally, Minnie stopped searching for jobs for which she was suited and decided to take anything that she could get: nursing home aide, telephone marketer, dishwasher, bingo attendant–any job that earned a little money and let her escape her mother's persistent nagging about mothering, housekeeping, drinking, or any of Minnie's other failings.

Minnie's eye problem didn't vanish with the cataract operation; instead, it got progressively worse. She was told that she would have to continue the injections that she so dreaded, and that she might need another operation to prevent her from going blind in one eye. The bifocals that came next acted as an inescapable reminder, especially whenever Minnie looked in the mirror.

Minnie was finding it increasingly difficult to maintain the self-confidence that had become her trademark among both friends and acquaintances. When her thyroid started to act up, it left her face bloated for anywhere from a few hours to several days. At these times she felt especially low, staying indoors and keeping her swollen face from public view. This was no easy feat when she was working or running errands. Sometimes she would ask her mother to go out instead, but Maggie was uncomfortable about leaving Roseanne with Minnie, an issue that further saddened Minnie. Sometimes Minnie would be so frustrated with her medical situation and with her mother that she would storm out of the apartment, draped in an oversize hat worn to draw attention away from her bifocals, a thick scarf covering the lower, swollen, part of her face, and her sister, Linda, in hand. A cute eight-year-old Indian usually succeeded in diverting people's attention, at least long enough for Minnie to throw some change on the counter and make her way out of the store with several bags of groceries shared between the two of them.

Minnie and Maggie Bugden kept in touch as best as they could. Before Minnie's return to Toronto, Maggie had left her job with the city and moved to Scarborough to be closer to her new job as a clerk for a ball-bearings manufacturer; Minnie and her family were living in the west end. Just as well—Minnie didn't like to invite people over when her mother was around.

Occasionally, Minnie and Maggie would meet for a meal, but these meetings were more random than regular. Minnie had started spending more time with Mary Hill, and Beatrice Jonah, Minnie's original roommate in Ottawa, was in town, too. When those three were set to go out drinking, Maggie felt like a tag-along who would only put a damper on the evening.

While Maggie found Minnie's behaviour at these times frustrating, she also enjoyed seeing Minnie in good spirits again. But good spirits for Minnie increasingly involved drinking, leaving the two friends with little in common. More than a few times, Maggie would spot Minnie on the street, her little legs pumping in their usual hurried manner. Maggie would charge up to her and jump right in front of her, knowing that Minnie couldn't see anything to the side. As excited as Maggie was to surprise her old friend, the joy of the moment disappeared when Minnie would barely say hello, peer over Maggie's head as if spotting a bus or streetcar in the distance, and tear off without another word.

Minnie and her daughter, mother, and sister left Toronto for Moose Factory in 1971. Shortly after, Maggie received a letter from Minnie: her mother had had a stroke. Her father had been offered a job as a maintenance man at the school in Kashechewan, a Cree reserve near Fort Albany. She and two-year-old Roseanne were going to stay in Moose Factory until a house was built for them on the reserve.

The following year, Maggie moved to Ottawa and lost touch with many of her old friends. She wondered about Minnie though, who had, once before, popped back into her life after seemingly being gone forever.

When several years passed and there was no letter from Kashechewan, Maggie wondered if Minnie's family ever actually moved there. A decade later, she was still wondering, but, by that time, Minnie Sutherland was a pleasant though distant memory. Maggie was convinced that Minnie was somewhere, married with five children and telling Crazy Eights partners tame versions of the captivating stories that she could never forget.

Chapter Ten

RESCUE

*She said that guys sleeping on benches
would take care of her.*
— MAGGIE BUGDEN

Just before Christmas 1986, Maggie received a distressing letter from Minnie. The letter, postmarked September and addressed in barely legible handwriting, had travelled as far as Jamaica before it finally made its way to Chisasibi, the reserve in Northern Quebec where Maggie was now staying with her family.

Maggie's first impulse was to call, but Minnie had given no telephone number, and she couldn't find a Minnie Sutherland listed in the Toronto directory. She drew on her recollection of memories that included Minnie and came up with the name Evelyn Mark. She hadn't spoken to Evelyn in two decades but easily found her telephone number through directory assistance. When she finally got talking to Evelyn, who hadn't heard from Minnie in years, she filled her in on the news.

Minnie had been kicked out of a rooming house off Church Street in Toronto. She was living on the street, staying wherever anyone had room or sleeping on a bench in one of the parks behind Yonge Street. She had made friends with a group of homeless people who panhandled on the busy part of Yonge between Dundas and Queen. She had another daughter, Violet, who was eight years old and living with her sister, Linda, and Linda's family in Kash. Roseanne was eighteen and going to school in Timmins. Minnie was having a hard time staying dry, but didn't want to go home. Her eyesight was deteriorating; she felt like giving up.

Could Maggie come and get a place with her?

Over the phone, Maggie and Evelyn agreed on how they should respond: Evelyn would send a letter through another native friend in Toronto, asking him to contact James Froh, the pastor of the Native People's Parish. They were sure that, despite her condition, Minnie would maintain some contact with the native community and would have kept in touch with James. If that effort failed, the friend was to go to Yonge Street and ask any natives living on the street if they had seen a little Cree woman with thick glasses.

Maggie's letter reached Minnie in January 1987. By that time, she was dry, living in a rooming house with about twenty other people, and taking a course in marketing. The letter expressed concern about her situation and told her to get out of Toronto as soon as she could, even if it meant going back to her mother and sister in Kashechewan. It also said that she was welcome to come to Ottawa: Evelyn was there and Maggie was moving back as well.

Minnie wrote back to Evelyn, telling her that she would come after she finished her course, in a few months.

Coroner's Inquest Testimony – Maggie Bugden

A. ...her eyesight got worse and when she moved here in Ottawa, she told me that she couldn't see from one eye, she lost one of her eyes.

Q. Um-hmm.

A. And the other eye, she told me that she–doesn't have a pupil...

Q. Um-hmm.

A. ...or something like that, that her eyes–her glasses were the only ones that could help her see.

In the years since her last contact with Minnie, Maggie had raised a daughter, Cita. Now fourteen, Cita had come to Ottawa and was living with her mother in a small studio apartment that was barely big enough for the two of them. Maggie had just enrolled in a ten-month word-processing course.

Evelyn had her own house in Vanier, so Maggie and Evelyn agreed that Minnie would stay there until she found her own place. Both women had witnessed, at one time or another, Minnie's strong desire for independence. They also knew that her efforts to be independent had not always been successful, and that for Minnie to write asking for help meant that she was in dire straits. When Minnie arrived, they knew they would have to express their invitation as a temporary arrangement only, until she could get back on her feet.

Minnie turned up later than expected: the last day of October 1987. She looked worn and bitter. Little of the pride that both Maggie and Evelyn had once admired in her was evident. There were no pretty clothes like the ones she used to wear. No brass lighter. No smell of Avon. Just a forty-year-old Indian who looked fifty, a second-hand grey outfit, a small vinyl purse, a scratched-up valise, and a pair of black-rimmed bifocals that seemed to cover half of her round, sallow face.

Maggie and Evelyn welcomed Minnie with all the enthusiasm they could muster, conscious of the fact that this was not the Minnie they once knew, and that Minnie felt their discomfort. They sat and talked at the bus station for a while, then walked up to Bank Street and treated her to dinner. She made a comment about how conservative Ottawa was compared to Toronto. Sinking into the booth, she smiled knowingly at her two quiet friends and thanked them for letting her come.

They took a bus back to Evelyn's place. The familiar route spurred Minnie's excitement and initiated a string of questions: "Is the Rat Hole still open?" she asked, remembering the Rialto Theatre, which got its nickname from the rodents that raced down the aisles under the projector's light. "Isn't that where the Oak Door used to be?" she wondered, recalling the bedroom prowess of one boy she had met there. And "Where's the Mocambo restaurant?" she demanded, peering through the window for a sign of it, until Evelyn told her it had been sold a few years back after the owners' teenage daughter had been killed in a car accident on the way to Florida. Minnie was silent for a moment, then mumbled that she would like to take Violet and go to Florida someday.

At Evelyn's place, they brought one another up to date on news from home. Minnie talked jubilantly about her best friend in Kash, Christy Wesley. She told them that her eldest daughter, Roseanne, was pregnant, and passed around recent pictures of Violet for her friends to gush over. She added a few words about her mother before reporting that her father was ill with cancer. After a delicate silence, the conversation shifted to the job market in Ottawa.

Evelyn was currently unemployed and couldn't give Minnie any ideas on where to start looking for work. Maggie, on the other hand, was full of suggestions about opportunities in the new world of computers. But Minnie's skills were social, not technical, and her eyesight, even with glasses, favoured neither keyboarding nor looking at a computer screen all day.

Babysitting was rejected the moment it was raised. Childcare was not for Minnie; it would only depress her further. She already felt guilty about being unable to take care of her own children. Despite everyone's reassurances about her love for her kids, and the likelihood that, one day, she would have Violet with her, the years of badgering from her mother had left Minnie insecure about her own mothering abilities. Evelyn and Maggie agreed that minding children other than her own would not relieve Minnie of her depression, even if it brought in some money.

Minnie was aware of the liability represented by her eyes, both in regard to appearance and practicality. She had a card from the Canadian National Institute for the Blind, but all it did was guarantee her a social welfare cheque and transportation privileges around town. To Minnie, it served little purpose except to label her *handicapped.* Minnie didn't want to single herself out, or to sponge off of society. She wanted to work.

Coroner's Inquest Testimony – Maggie Bugden

A. So she didn't feel confident to go and look for a job because of her eyesight, you know...so I told her I'll–I'll go with you and I'll support you, so let's look onto those little cards that they have there, and so she applied for a job as a health care aide, and I believe it was the Manpower that gave her a–a–to go to that Salem programme where she attended some kind of programme so that she could get back in the work force...That's when she worked at the Dalhousie Centre, after she graduated from the programme.

Minnie's return to the ranks of the employed also marked her resurgence in the social scene. In no time at all, Minnie was calling everyone whose name she could remember from her last stint in Ottawa, and renewing acquaintances with people she knew from Kash, including her cousins Doreen Milbury, Doreen's husband, Tim, and Doreen's sister, Joyce Wesley. The Saturday after she started work at the Dalhousie Health and Community Services Centre, Minnie, Doreen, and a few other women celebrated Minnie's new job by heading out for an evening of their absolute favourite pastime: Bingo.

It was great to be back in Ottawa.

I called Joyce and said "she's still not home." That's when Joyce told me her side of the story.

— DOREEN MILBURY

Had they known of her situation in the early days of January 1989, any number of people who had the opportunity of meeting Minnie, either at work or through social circles, would have rushed to her side at the Ottawa General Hospital. But most of them had not seen Minnie in months–not since she had lost her job at the Dalhousie Centre–and even those closest to her–Evelyn, Maggie, and Doreen–didn't know she was in the hospital.

One of the hospital's social workers had tried for three days running to find Minnie's next of kin. All the woman had at her disposal was the admission file that noted Minnie's name, the names of two physicians she had seen previously–one in Toronto, the other in Moose Factory–and a notation that her personal belongings consisted of a coat, a tuque, some beat-up old clothes, and a purse. The purse, which was with her upon her arrival in Emergency, could not be found.

Neither of the two doctors Minnie had seen in past years were able to provide any useful information on the whereabouts of her family. Yes, she had been to see them, but the telephone numbers and forwarding addresses she had left led nowhere.

The social worker called directory assistance in several northern towns where natives have traditionally lived, asking for a listing for a Minnie Sutherland. She eventually found an E. Sutherland in Moosonee, but the shy voice on the other end of the line said that she was only distantly related to the Ottawa Minnie

Sutherland. However, she knew of a daughter, Roseanne, living in Timmins.

Roseanne was perplexed by the call. "Your mother was found in a snowbank." She knew her mother had a long history of various illnesses, but this time it sounded serious. "She's in intensive care." Could it be something like a stroke or a heart attack?, she wondered. "You may want to come down." But Roseanne knew that her mother was resilient. Surely she would be strutting out of the hospital any day, telling all of them that she was fine and that, thankfully, she'd lost five pounds as a result of the ordeal.

Roseanne called her aunt Linda with the news—*Linda would know what to do.*

The family discussed the situation and decided that Linda and her husband, John, would make the trip to Ottawa. They agreed that Roseanne, now a mother, had her hands full with the baby and school exams about to start. Sidney, older brother to Minnie and Linda, had his store to run, and, besides, he wouldn't set foot on a plane. And mother Maggie, though over the worst part of mourning her husband Bart's death that fall, was waiting on a call from the hospital in Moose Factory for surgery to remove a gangrenous leg. And she was blind.

Linda called cousin Doreen in Ottawa and told her that Minnie was in the hospital. Doreen was puzzled; she had spoken to her sister, Joyce, just yesterday, and Joyce had been telling her about the good time she and Minnie had at the Claude Tavern on New Year's Eve. She hadn't mentioned anything about Minnie's being sick. But the news explained why there had been no answer at Minnie's apartment all New Year's Day and the day after—Minnie hadn't shacked up with some Chinese guy after all.

Doreen assured Linda that her husband, Tim, would pick her and John up at the airport. Then she called Joyce to tell her that Minnie was in the hospital. She asked if Joyce had noticed anything wrong on New Year's Eve. Joyce simply replied that Minnie had been pretty drunk that night.

Minnie remained unconscious for several days after being admitted to the hospital. During that time, a senior resident, Dr. Paul Hébert, and an intern ordered numerous blood tests. They reviewed the results and ruled out a drug overdose, which was a plausible explanation for a person found unconscious in a snowbank on New Year's Eve.

A CT scan of Minnie's brain had been taken. To Dr. Hébert, the results appeared normal. But the staff neurosurgeon, Dr. Jean-Maurice Dennery, thought differently, noticing a stenosis, or narrowing, of the channel that connects the back and front of the brain and that serves to conduct the cerebrospinal fluid.

Knowing that Dr. Dennery wanted further tests taken, Dr. Gabriel Khan, the physician in charge of the emergency room on January 2, turned the case over to him. He also arranged with Dr. Gwynne Jones, the hospital's Intensive Care Unit coordinator, to have Minnie moved to that unit.

Dr. Jones and his team were perplexed about the cause of Minnie's illness. The level of alcohol in her blood appeared to have contributed to her condition, but probably not to any great extent. A low level of phenobarbitone was also in her blood, raising the likelihood that Minnie had been on anticonvulsant medication. Had she not been taking it as prescribed? With no diagnosis, there were other questions as well.

Coroner's Inquest Testimony – Dr. Gwynne Jones

A. There was a question of diabetes. There was changes within the eyes seen, and although the blood sugar was not elevated, it was a question of whether there had been a change in the blood sugar that had caused this.

In addition, the samples had been taken from the fluid surrounding the brain, which were abnormal, showing evidence of some red blood cells, and this had been interpreted at this time as—as trauma caused by putting the needle in, and that may well have been the case.

In addition, there was some white blood cells within
this, and there was a question of whether this could
have been meningitis. In addition, we had the opin-
ion of Dr. Dennery that the—that the ventricles, the
fluid-containing cavities in the head were very dilat-
ed, and that he had felt that this was most likely
a—a—a narrowing of the—of the drainage tube, the
aqueduct that Dr. Khan mentioned that this was
likely congenital abnormality and that the dilation of
the—of these ventricles and the pressure that this
was inducing had caused this problem, but it was
also possible that this had been present for many
years and that a—an infection or a convulsion had
been then the final straw that had made—brought her
into this condition.

Q. All right.

A. In view of her changes within the eyes, the suggestion of diabetes and perhaps detached retinas with
laser therapy, it was felt that she—people with diabetes and people of native Indian extraction, have
a—have a higher prevalence for tuberculosis, and for
this reason, T.B. of the meninges was considered a
possibility and this can, indeed, cause this stenosis
of the aqueduct, and so she was at this time treated
for the—for a possible meningitis, as it was felt that
perhaps it was entirely due to the aqueduct stenosis,
but that we couldn't miss this diagnosis.

Patrick Smith and Michel Filion, two of the three university
students who witnessed Minnie's accident, were readying themselves for a trip to Acapulco they had planned months before. The
Christmas holidays were over, and the coldest part of the winter
was about to begin. Those Ottawans who couldn't afford a winter
vacation South envied people like Patrick and Michel, who would
return in a week flaunting a tan.

Patrick had never stopped thinking about the events that had
occurred in front of J. R. Dallas early New Year's Day. The rage he
felt over the officers' treatment of Minnie had imprinted the

events of that night. Yet, his friend Michel had to remind him of their promise to call Joyce, and that three days had already passed.

Joyce was out when Patrick called on the morning of January 3. Her husband, Billy, said that she would be back in the evening.

Patrick introduced himself and explained the purpose of his call: he and his friends had been in Hull on New Year's Eve, had seen Minnie get hit by a car on Principale, and had helped Joyce bring her into a restaurant. Billy said that he and Joyce had only just heard that Minnie was in hospital in serious condition. Her sister, Linda, was flying down from James Bay to see her. He didn't know which hospital, but maybe Joyce would. He seemed surprised to hear that there had been an accident.

When Joyce arrived home later that day, Billy told her that a Patrick Smith had called. Was it true that Minnie had been hit by a car?

Patrick called again later in the day and spoke to Joyce. She confirmed that, indeed, Minnie was in hospital and was, apparently, in serious condition. Patrick asked if Joyce had ever called an ambulance that night. She said no. He asked if she had seen Minnie in the hospital or if she was going to see her, but Joyce again said no; she didn't even know which hospital Minnie was in. Did the hospital know Minnie had been hit by a car? Joyce didn't know.

Coroner's Inquest Testimony – Patrick Smith

A. ...I have, like, a directory of all the hospitals, so I–I started calling around to the hospitals...and I found her at the General. That's where it was, and a nurse actually–I got right up to her ward, they put me right up to her ward and some–I had called–I was talking to this nurse and she said, like, she freaked, she couldn't believe I actually knew what had happened to her, you know, like she–she said–and anyway, I said, "Yeah, she was hit by a car in Hull."

Patrick's information didn't help to determine what was wrong with Minnie, nor did it explain why, after four days, she was still unconscious. It did, however, convince the doctors to discontinue treating Minnie for tuberculosis and meningitis.

Minnie underwent a further examination to ensure that no other injuries were evident. Hospital staff took detailed X-rays of her spine and limbs, and couldn't find evidence of trauma elsewhere in her body. The now known possibility of trauma to the head made more sense of the diagnosis toward which they had been inching: the narrowing of the duct in the brain had probably existed for a long time, but the trauma had caused some swelling.

After the fourth of January, Minnie's condition improved steadily. She had not fully regained consciousness, but she was beginning to respond to a variety of stimuli. By the time Linda arrived on the sixth and discovered the details of how her sister ended up in hospital, Minnie was able to move her lips to mouth what Linda believed to be "hello." She was also breathing more comfortably, though with the aid of the ventilator to which she had been hooked up since her admission.

The next day, Minnie was able to open her eyes. Her mouth was busy practising sounds, but the tube in her throat rendered each utterance little more than a gurgle. John and Linda could tell by the attempt to speak, along with the sudden intensity of her breathing, that Minnie was happy to see them. Knowing that Minnie always found the positive in adverse situations, they wondered what was going on in her mind right now: without the medication and the equipment hooked up inside and around her, surely she would have let loose a stream of exclamations about the trouble she had gotten herself into this time.

Dr. Jones discussed with Dr. Dennery the possibility of moving her out of intensive care sometime in the next few days. Dr. Dennery agreed, providing they continue to investigate the effect of the accident on what they were convinced was a congenital problem with her brain.

The doctors assured Linda that Minnie's condition was serious, though likely not life-threatening. She questioned their prognosis the following day when she came to visit. In the twenty-four hours since she and John had arrived, Minnie had truly begun to look better—sufficiently so that Linda decided it was best for them to leave. They both had jobs to get back to; John's at the Kash airport, hers at the reserve school board. There were their four children and Violet, who, while they were away, were staying with one of John's sisters. And there was Maggie, probably their greatest concern, for she wouldn't leave the house while they were away, determined to get around on her own yet dependent on everyone around her to keep her company and run her errands.

Before they left, Linda insisted that once Minnie was out of the hospital, she would come back down and take care of her. The idea had planted itself in her mind the moment she saw Minnie lying so still in the hospital bed. Absent was Minnie's usual spunk; lost was her ability to smile under the most difficult circumstances. Linda had realized then that something would have to change if Minnie was to survive in the world that so inspired her.

Linda also knew that, short of binding and gagging Minnie for the trip back, it would be pointless to try to persuade her sister to stay put in Kash, despite the condition she may be in. She also knew that as long as Minnie's little legs could stir, they would be moving her out of Kash and away from their mother. Unprepared to lose her big sister to the lures of any city, Linda came to the conclusion that Minnie needed a big sister now. She and John and the kids would simply have to move to Ottawa.

Linda hugged Minnie goodbye, withholding tears until she was on her way out the door. John stayed a little longer, thinking about how the dear person lying in the hospital bed had been treated by the authorities.

He asked Minnie a few questions, telling her to squeeze his

hand once for *yes* and two times for *no*. "Do you know where you are?" One squeeze. "Do you know what day it is?" Two squeezes. "Do you know you were hit by a car?" One.

Still holding on to Minnie's hand, John asked Minnie if she knew she had been wronged. This time she nodded her head.

Chapter Twelve
ECHOES

There was no unifying diagnosis...our role at that time was to support her as best we could to ensure healing.
— Dr. Gwynne Jones

News of Minnie's illness and the circumstances that had put her in the hospital rapidly spread through Kashechewan the evening before John and Linda left for Ottawa. Their urgent call to Air Creebec, which resulted in two booked passengers being bumped to another flight, quickly became the prime topic of discussion in Kash.

In many native communities, news that one of its own is in the hospital is usually met with as much (or as little) surprise as a report that the same person is in jail. So often, loved ones return from places like Toronto, Ottawa, and Winnipeg with grim tales of neglect and prejudice. That their people end up in hospitals and prisons during their bouts of adventure in these cities ceased to be shocking news long ago.

The people of Kashechewan had no such predispositions. In fact, if Linda returned with news that Minnie was flying back the next day to recover in Kash, there would be cause for alarm. Far better medical care existed in a city like Ottawa than in the types of hospitals found in towns like Moose Factory and Moosonee, let alone in a solitary nurse's station in Kashechewan.

In the minds of Kash residents, there was always conflict between criticizing the evils of the city and condoning its benefits. As long as Minnie remained in an urban institution, she would receive better medical care than possibly anywhere else. In the minds of everyone on the reserve, however, as long as she pursued a life in one of Canada's big cities, all of which had a history of treating native people differently than whites, her fate would remain precarious.

Upon the Wynnes' return the following evening, the first person to learn that "Minnie is going to be okay," was the watchman at the airport gate. After that it didn't take long for the message to travel through the community. It spread via residents picking up other passengers from the same flight. It became the topic of conversation among airport workers who had no other work to do once the plane had landed. It was discussed in the various confectionaries when passengers and airport staff stopped on their way home to pick up Coke, potato chips, and other staples of life on the reserve.

Most people expressed immediate relief upon hearing that Minnie was better, especially when Linda described the excellent care her sister seemed to be getting at the Ottawa General Hospital. The older people around Kash gave thanks to God, and to Linda and John for making the trip to check things out.

When the good news reached Minnie's mother, all the tension and emotional exhaustion that had built up in the last twenty-four hours was washed away. Above all, Maggie was relieved, and displayed it by suggesting that they have some tea and talk about what to do next. Despite her firm and sometimes ugly temperament, Maggie could command warmth and gaiety in the household. Tonight, she told stories of other people who had been sick and recovered, sang familiar hymns, and made everyone feel good about the home in which they lived.

Christy Wesley called the moment Linda got in the door. From her front porch, she had heard a truck roll by ten minutes or so after the flight from Timmins was scheduled to come in, and had already heard from someone in the village that John and Linda were headed back. She waited the few minutes it would take them to make their way home before she picked up the phone and dialled.

Though five years her junior, Christy was Minnie's best friend in Kashechewan. Born in Moose Factory, but adopted as a baby and brought to Kash by an elderly Cree woman named Lola, Christy regarded the little settlement on the bank of the Albany River as her home. When Minnie's family moved there fifteen years later, Christy quickly became friends with the bouncy girl who everyone said couldn't stay in one place for very long. Though Minnie had different mannerisms and ideals, Christy opened her heart to the little ball of fire who, if not for the gravel and dust in Kash, would favour patent-leather spikes and sequined dresses to the sneakers and sweatshirts commonly worn on the reserve.

From the start, Christy was dazzled by Minnie's self-confidence. Here was an Indian with class, a Cree woman comfortable walking around in shorts and a halter top—something other than the jeans and sweatshirts that Christy and many of the other women in Kash almost always wore. Unlike nearly all the other women that Christy knew, Minnie was not afraid to talk about things like depression, desperation, or sex. Minnie was not the most physically attractive woman on the reserve, but she rarely associated with people to whom outer beauty mattered. Rather, she clung to the outcasts of Kash society, people for whom understanding words meant more than a pretty face.

Other women on the reserve wondered what drew Minnie and Christy together, and referred to them as salt and pepper, a label more suited to the way they complemented each other than to their differing characters. Christy was an introvert, shy and distrustful of strangers, particularly whites; Minnie was an extrovert who went out of her way to talk to everyone, especially whites and Asian men. Christy was content with the quiet of life on the reserve; Minnie resented that existence. Christy met a man in Kash to whom she would remain loyal forever; Minnie left the reserve whenever she could to search for a relationship in which she had some say.

Christy was married to Joyce Wesley's older brother, David, but had never become especially close to Joyce. In fact, none of her family relationships, including those with in-laws, or her own cousins, could compare to the special bond she shared with Minnie.

Only Minnie could make Christy's head spin with fantastic stories about a world more interesting and free than hers would ever be. Often, while Minnie entertained a group of friends with stories about life in Toronto, Christy would sit quietly among them, wondering what it would be like to live there, free of all her inhibitions.

After the stories ended and the group dispersed, Christy would see a subtle change in Minnie. The girl who, minutes before, could ridicule her listeners' home and make them laugh would shed her public persona and become sentimental about being home. It always made Christy wonder if, this time, Minnie was back to stay. But by the end of a day spent with her mother, Minnie would be making plans to leave as soon as she could get the money together.

What impressed Christy most about Minnie was that she rarely complained—what she didn't like she tried to change. She sought adventure, and got it, rationalizing that even the most disastrous trips—the ones that broke her financially and forced her to depend on her family once again—taught her something.

Regardless of the reasons for her return or the length of time she'd been gone, Minnie and Christy could pick up right where they left off, with Minnie telling her quiet friend new stories about the city and making her blush at some of the more fantastic escapades. When it came to catching up on the whereabouts of mutual friends in the city or the status of a relative's son or daughter who had run away, Minnie would try to change the subject. She never had the heart to tell her innocent friend that the last time she saw *this* man from Moosonee, he'd been passed out drunk at Yonge and Dundas, or that when she last saw *that* girl from Moose Factory, she was living off an ugly old white man to keep herself off the streets.

Minnie was going to be okay.

When David got home, Christy told him the news that he had already picked up on the way. Like Christy, he was relieved: *Of course Minnie would be okay; she always landed on her feet.* They joked about the stories Minnie would bring back about this New Year's Eve.

ℒ♪

From the reserve office, Kashechewan's chief, Jonathan Solomon, saw John Wynne's truck pass by. He had heard that they were scheduled to return home that day and was anxious to hear about Minnie. Though he tried, he could not make out the expression on John's face, just the typically serene profile jouncing up and down, half screened by the cloud of fumes billowing up from the rear of the truck. "I hope it's good news," he thought, after recalling the fate of too many of his people who had left the reserve to explore the "other" world.

Despite his efforts to train young people to survive when they got to the city—how to get settled, who to contact, where to get cheap clothes, where to start looking for a job—he couldn't understand the allure of leaving the security of the reserve to live with a people who had betrayed your ancestors so brutally. Did any of them really believe that they would be accepted as equals once outside their native communities? He despaired at the prospect of the many others who would also leave in the months and years to come. They, too, sought a better, more prosperous life elsewhere.

Jonathan contemplated the plight of his people, then called Linda. *Minnie was going to be okay.* He asked when she would be coming home.

Other than Linda and John, Minnie had no visitors during her stay at the Ottawa General. Tim Milbury, Doreen's husband, had made an attempt to see her, but was not allowed into her room because he was not immediate family. No one else showed up.

The twenty years since Minnie had first moved to Ottawa was

too long a time to maintain relationships. A few of Minnie's Ottawa friends from 1966 were still in the city, but they didn't even know Minnie had moved back there, let alone that she was in the hospital. She had tried to look them up when she arrived, but hadn't been able to connect, likely because many of them had unlisted numbers, were married with new names, or like herself, didn't stay in one place for long. That Evelyn Mark and Maggie Bugden were both in Ottawa when Minnie planned her return was pure coincidence; both women had also spent extended periods elsewhere. Had Minnie chosen to return to Ottawa just one year earlier, neither of her two old friends would have been there to welcome her.

ཤཕ

Maggie didn't know anything about Minnie being in the hospital until Evelyn stopped by her place on the sixth of January. Maggie had been calling Minnie's apartment since New Year's Day and had become increasingly worried each time the phone went unanswered. Fifteen years earlier, she would have assumed that Minnie had spontaneously decided to head back north, but not this time. Something else had to have happened. After all, they had spoken before the holidays and Minnie hadn't seemed homesick. Actually, she had said she was glad not to be in Kash this first Christmas since her father's death. She'd been lonely for some male companionship, but that wasn't anything new.

The way Evelyn described it, neither the accident nor Minnie's hospitalization sounded too serious, and so Maggie was surprised to hear that Linda had travelled all the way from Kash just to see her. Evelyn explained that in the beginning the prognosis was grave, but a change for the better in Minnie's condition suggested that she was going to be all right. Maggie wanted to hear details about the accident, but Evelyn had little information to offer, as she had barely seen Minnie after they had entered J.R.'s together that night.

ཤཕ

In addition to her two best friends, Minnie had a few relatives—mostly distant ones—living in Ottawa, but she had only kept in touch with one—her cousin and bingo partner Doreen Milbury. Doreen believed that Minnie was on the mend and would soon be out of the hospital. At least that's the impression she got from Linda. Her thoughts were confirmed by Joyce, who told her that she didn't think Minnie was really hurt by the car; probably just knocked out from the fall. *She was pretty drunk.*

Weakened by muscular dystrophy and dependent on a wheelchair to get around, Doreen felt that getting herself to the hospital would have meant a major effort on her husband's part: getting her into and out of the car to go there, then back into it, and out of the car again when they returned home. Tim said he didn't mind taking her, but felt that it was better to let the doctors take care of Minnie now. Doreen would see Minnie when she was better, probably at bingo.

❧

The social services department at the Ottawa General Hospital had received another request for help concerning Minnie Sutherland. They had first been called upon to locate Minnie's next of kin and, at the same time, to obtain some information on her medical history, if possible. These requests were common when people were admitted alone and inebriated in the early hours of the morning. But the request received on January 6 was different, something they had never previously dealt with or anticipated. Since Patrick Smith's call to the hospital with information about Minnie being hit by a car in Hull, the urgency placed on finding relatives and medical history suddenly shifted to determining how hard she was hit, how hard she fell, and why, instead of bringing her to a hospital, the police officers on the scene had left her in a snowbank.

The social worker who two days earlier had located Minnie's sister, Linda, called Hull police headquarters several times the day after Patrick Smith notified the hospital of the accident. A request to speak with either of the two officers at the scene was met with silence, followed by a half-English, half-French explanation that callers are not permitted to speak directly with officers.

Although the social worker explained that an emergency existed, she was asked to leave a number so that one of the sergeants could call back. After leaving a detailed message, which the attendant seemed to have difficulty understanding, she waited. Several hours passed without word, prompting the head of the social services department to make a second call, this time stating the absolute necessity of obtaining information about the accident, warning that the media may be called in for the search, and demanding that someone in charge immediately call Dr. Gwynne Jones at the Ottawa General Hospital.

It wasn't until the next day, January 7, that Captain Armand Caron of the Hull police met with Dr. Jones. He expressed deep regret over the incident, then relief once he heard that Minnie was getting well. He said he was aware of an episode on New Year's Eve concerning an intoxicated native woman who fell on rue Principale, but he absolved his officers of any real involvement except in helping the fallen woman to the side of the road. Dr. Jones, however, was puzzled by how familiar the sergeant was with the events that followed a *fall*. And since it was the doctor's understanding that the police officers had driven away after "helping" Minnie to the side of the road, how could Captain Caron possibly have known then that three young men, whose names he also knew, escorted Minnie and Joyce into a restaurant? Moreover, how did he know that three unidentified men took Minnie—and Joyce—to Ottawa? It was apparent that the Hull Police Department, with Captain Caron at the helm, were particularly interested in what they kept referring to as simply an "incident."

At the beginning of her second week in the hospital, there was a marked improvement in Minnie's condition. She could move her limbs and was able to express herself, either by grunting a preference or gesturing her rejection of something put before her, particularly another needle or feeding tube. She still couldn't breathe without the aid of a ventilator, but the doctors were confident that they could remove it in a day or two. Most of the tests recently conducted were positive, showing that the swelling in Minnie's brain was subsiding.

With the exception of Chief of Neurology Dr. Robert Nelson, the hospital's physicians were convinced that Minnie had an underlying, chronic abnormality in her brain, and that this abnormality had been aggravated by a bang to the head, likely from her falling on the road and hitting her head on the asphalt. There was still some question about whether the chronic problem or the trauma had most influenced her incapacitation, but the answer didn't seem to matter that much—she appeared well on her way to a complete recovery.

Notation on Minnie Sutherland's medical file by
Dr. Nelson, January 7, 1989
This lady is still undiagnosed as far as I am concerned. She is fairly alert and moves her limbs, and the right hand. Her right toes move, but slightly less so on the left. And the reflexes of the feet are not diagnostic. The limbs are loose and not spastic or increased in tone, and the scan, this is the second scan, shows blood in the ventricles. And we now see the proximal aqueduct but I don't see the fourth ventricle. Does she have a posterior fossa mass? She has a short neck. Could she have an anomaly, and a congenital abnormality of the craniocervical junction? And she also has a very high protein level in the cerebrospinal fluid. Possibly the motor vehicle accident has caused trauma of the upper cervical spine and this must be X-rayed. In addition, an MRI.

In 1989, Magnetic Resonance Imaging—MRI—provided the most sophisticated anatomical picture of the human brain and spine. Because the technology was new and the Ottawa General had one of only two such scanners in the entire city, the waiting list for an MRI scan was daunting–weeks for some outpatients, and days for in-patients not deemed to be in critical condition. Hospital policy stated that only emergency situations could bump a patient from their coveted position on the list.

Coroner's Inquest–Cross-Examination –
Dr. Gwynne Jones

Q. And was this test ever done?

A. The test was never done. It was planned to be done, but it was never–it–was never done. In view of her clinical improvement, it was felt that–that, obviously, there's a waiting list for these things, and it was felt that the urgency to remove some–was not severe–it was not severe enough–it was not great enough to remove somebody else from the–from the list. Obviously, that was not wise.

On January 9, Dr. Jones ordered Minnie to be moved from the intensive care unit to the neurosurgery observation area. The ventilator was removed, and she was breathing normally without it. She was also beginning to speak, although the swelling in her vocal cords continued to make it painful for her to talk.

In her room that evening, a new catheter was inserted into Minnie via her shoulder in an attempt to reach a vein large enough to receive the line that would feed medication and fluids into her system and test for gases in her blood. An hour or two after the procedure, a technician looking at a recent X-ray realized that the catheter was not hooked up to a vein at all, but had been inserted into an artery.

Once the catheter was properly reconnected–to a vein this time–Minnie fell asleep easily, exhausted from the move earlier that day, the repeated search for veins into which the nurses could stick needles, and an unremitting pressure in her head.

It was after one o'clock on the morning of January 11 when the telephone rang, waking both Doreen and Tim Milbury. The lady on the other end of the line introduced herself as a nurse from the Ottawa General Hospital and asked Doreen if she was Minnie Sutherland's cousin. Doreen said yes, she was her cousin, and asked if Minnie was okay. The nurse said that Minnie wasn't doing very well and inquired if Doreen could come to the hospital as soon as possible. When Doreen asked what was wrong, all the nurse would tell her was, "We've just spoken to Linda, and she suggested we call you. Can you come down as soon as possible?"

Tim helped Doreen to the side of the bed and into her wheelchair. She suggested that he go alone, saying that the call sounded urgent and that he could get there faster if he didn't have to wait for her to get ready. But Tim reminded her that the nurses hadn't let him see Minnie when Linda and John were there, and that was when she was getting better. "Why would they let me in now?"

Doreen was just pulling on her coat when the telephone rang again. Tim answered this time. It was Linda. After a brief exchange, he passed the receiver to Doreen, his expression puzzled.

Linda asked, "Did the hospital just call you?"

"Yeah, they just called," Doreen responded nervously. "I think Minnie's taken a turn. We're just leaving."

Linda told her there was no point. Minnie had just died.

It was like a dream...like a mirror
shattering in my mind.
— LINDA WYNNE

Letter to Hull police from Dr. Gwynne Jones, January 17, 1989

It is with great regret that I must write of the unfortunate case of Mrs. [sic] Minnie Sutherland who was
admitted to the Ottawa General Hospital on January
the first, 1989, and died on June [sic] the 11th, as a
result of a blood clot in the back of the brain sustained
during an accident in the early hours of January the
first. Her admission to the intensive care unit followed
a period of investigation in the emergency room. The
patient had arrived in the emergency room without
any history whatsoever and with no friends or relatives accompanying her. Thus, no past medical history
or evidence of recent illness or injury was available.
As a result, the initial investigations included assess-
ments for drug overdose and serious infection. Initial
brain scans showed enlargement of the spinal fluid
containing chambers, ventricles in keeping with hydro-
cephalus, but no other abnormalities to suggest other
damage to the brain.

In view of this finding and of the abnormalities within
the brain fluid, treatment with a drain to release pressure and antibiotics to cover meningitis were under-
taken. She was brought to the intensive care unit for
artificial ventilation as it had been necessary to insert
a tube into her larynx to ensure adequate breathing.

She remained in this state of deep coma with signs of raised pressure in the brain over the next few days.

Later, it was possible to call her family doctor and family and obtain some past history but this did not help us elucidate the cause of all of these abnormalities.

On January the 3rd, we received a telephone call from Mr. Patrick Smith who was a witness to the accident and had heard that Mrs. Sutherland had been admitted to the Ottawa General Hospital. He called to inquire about her condition and was amazed to find that we knew nothing about the accident in Hull. He explained that Minnie had tried to cross the road on the Promenade du Portage and had been hit by a car and fell backwards. The driver of the car and her friend immediately stopped and got out of the car to see if Minnie was all right. These people were nurses. Mr. Smith and his friend also went to see if she was all right. The Hull Police arrived within minutes to investigate. According to Mr. Smith, the police instructed the two nurses to leave, then went to move Mrs. Sutherland. Mr. Smith suggested that the police not move Mrs. Sutherland until the ambulance arrived lest there'd been any severe injury for which movement could be dangerous. Mr. Smith stated that Mrs. Sutherland smelled of alcohol.

Mr. Smith alleged that the police officer asked them to leave rather brusquely. He then observed the police officers pick up Mrs. Sutherland and move her roughly into a snowbank.

Further details of the evening have been gleaned from other sources. It appears that Mrs. Sutherland woke up and she and her friend went across the road to a coffee bar. Within the coffee bar, Mrs. Sutherland felt nauseated and vomited twice. Some other people in the coffee bar asked if they could take Mrs. Sutherland to her home. This was agreed upon and the driver thought that Mrs. Sutherland lived on Laurier Street. On arrival in Laurier Street, Minnie was shown to be more inarticulate and drowsy. She was unable to find her apartment.

Mrs. Sutherland's friend then took Mrs. Sutherland out of the car and they walked up and down Laurier Street to keep the patient awake. 911 was called and the police arrived soon afterwards. It appeared that an ambulance also arrived, but it was decided that Mrs. Sutherland should go to the Ottawa General Hospital room in the police car. Here, she arrived alone and with no history available to the emergency physicians, as I have stated.

The course of Mrs. Sutherland's illness within the intensive care unit was one of gradual improvement. She was discharged up to the neurosurgery observation area and again was making a steady recovery until a sudden deterioration occurred in the early hours of January 11th, followed by a cardiac arrest, from which resuscitation was unsuccessful.

There is no doubt that the lack of information about the traumatic event was of great significance in making the initial diagnosis of the abnormality and in following this up to a logical conclusion which may have been able to prevent her demise.

It is also unfortunate that Mrs. Sutherland received powerful antibiotics for her condition which would not have been necessary had this history been available. The antibiotics do have their own particular risks.

In particular, if the allegations of the conduct of the Hull Police are correct, then a serious error of judgement has been made by the officers concerned and this should be investigated.

The morning of January 11, Linda readied her house for the visitors that would stop by their bungalow that day. With the children's help, she tidied up, clearing the floor of toys and collecting video cassettes from the tables in the living room. Each person in the household who was old enough to walk was asked to put away clothes in closets and drawers, and to make sure all the beds were neatly made. In the front entrance, room was made to store visitors' boots and hang coats. In the kitchen, two teapots were taken from the top cupboards and a dozen of the best cups and saucers set out.

As visitor after visitor stopped by, Linda felt all eyes on her. Disbelieving eyes. Pained eyes. Eyes that demanded an explanation.

Several hours before, Linda was informed of the hard fact that her sister had suffered a heart attack and died. HEART ATTACK. The more she thought about it, the less sense it made. Each time she explained the cause of Minnie's death to the friends that stopped by, Minnie's absence became more real to her, but her death didn't make any more sense.

The finality of the situation hit Linda with each word of sympathy. Her plans for a new life with Minnie in Ottawa seemed to have been part of a cruel dream. Now there was only a funeral to plan.

Coroner's Inquest Testimony – Dr. Vitale Montpetit

A. It was a fairly extensive fracture, extending all along the base of the posterior fossa and then along the suture line between the parietal–parietal and occipital bone.

Q. And just referring to yourself, is this at the back of the head that you found this?

A. Yes.

Q. And where in the back of the head would this be about?

A. In the posterior fossa, if you want me to...

Q. Just indicate sir on...

A. In this region here.

Q. All right. Sort of the upper back of the head.

A. Left posterior part of the head.

Q. All right. And is this like a fracture? Would this be like a hairline type of fracture that....

A. In this case, it was.

Q. All right.

A. Except that in the more posterior part, it seemed to follow the suture line between the parietal and occipital bones.

Q. All right. It followed the path where two bones had joined.

A. Where bone would join when it matures.

Q. All right and how long was the fracture, approximately, in inches?

A. About five to six inches.

What landed Minnie in hospital in Ottawa had never been clear to anyone in Kash. It wasn't that Linda tried to keep things quiet, it was just that the information she gleaned from the doctors, and collected from conversations with Joyce and Doreen, didn't amount to very much. Now that Minnie was dead, the demand for details took on a terrible urgency. Linda was desperate to explain how Minnie, who was, to all appearances, getting better, had suddenly died from a heart attack. How could she tell the relatives and friends that would stream into her house that day what had happened when she didn't know herself?

What happened to Minnie after she and John had left the hospital, anyway? She couldn't even begin to look for answers without descending into guilt: guilt for not being there; guilt for not bringing Minnie back with her.

And what about the morning Minnie was hit by the car? Where were her friends that she raved so much about? The authorities—what were they doing while her sister was in such obvious need of help? And where was their cousin Joyce after everyone else deserted Minnie?

In an attempt to sort things out, Linda turned over the events of her sister's New Year's Eve in her mind. What resulted were more questions and few answers.

Minnie had been hit by a car outside a bar in Hull.
 — *Had she been drinking?*
The police dragged her off the road and left her in a snowbank.
 — *Wasn't anyone else there?*
She and Joyce bummed a ride back to Ottawa.
 — *With whom?*
The Ottawa police thought Minnie was drunk.
 — *Was she?*
Joyce left her with the Ottawa police.
 — *Was Joyce drunk?*
She ended up at the hospital at six that morning.
 — *What took so long?*
The hospital didn't know she was hit by a car until four days later.
 — *Why didn't Joyce tell them?*

Coroner's Inquest Testimony – Joyce Wesley

Q. What did you do when you heard that she was in the hospital?

A. Nothing.

Q. O.K. Did you phone the hospital?

A. No.

Q. Did you go and see her?

A. No.

Q. All right. Did you give the hospital any kind of information or...?

A. No.

Between sobs and sniffles, Maggie Sutherland remained silent for the better part of the day, making the rest of the family long for the soothing voice that had spoken comforting words when tragedy struck other families in Kashechewan. But there was no engaging version of "By the Sweet By and By," and no inspirational reading of *The Old Rugged Cross*. Instead, she just sat and cried, once in a while navigating the kitchen with her white cane and offering to help Linda serve a cake or set out sandwiches that neighbours had brought over earlier in the day.

Once the guests were gone, Maggie's tears finally gave way to anger over the odd turn of events that had resulted in her daughter's death. Roseanne's arrival from Timmins proved to be the perfect antidote for everyone's tension; her reassuring words to Violet made everyone feel more secure. But then Sidney, Linda and Minnie's older brother, started to discuss Minnie's way of life with his mother, and began a barrage of criticism about how Minnie had sealed her own fate with the drinking and moving around she did.

No one tried to stop his ranting; it was best to remain silent and let him talk himself out. Finally he relented, leaving the house quiet once more, save for everyone's crying and the occasional bang of Maggie's cane whenever her frustration about being blind collided with her pain over her daughter's death.

Coroner's Inquest Testimony – Dr. Vitale Montpetit

A. Only on internal examination did we see there were contusions of the skull, both in the right frontal and left parietal/occipital region.

Q. All right.

A. Now, to sustain fracture at the base of the skull of that nature you'd need a severe blow. What I cannot explain in this case is which one is the coup and contre-coup. In other words, was she hit over the right frontal area and then fell backwards on the left side, or was she hit here and banged herself on the right frontal lobe, right frontal part of the skull, I cannot tell.

When Linda called Christy that morning to give her the news, the conversation was brief; she and Christy were women of few words at the best of times. They both knew that the time to share their feelings would come after all the duty calls had been made and visitors stopped coming to the Wynne household. After they spoke, Christy went about her usual morning chores–in the days to follow, the two women would make a point of stealing a few minutes away from their families to share the loss of someone they both loved.

For Christy, it was impossible to believe that someone who relished life as much as Minnie could be dead, no matter how cavalier her lifestyle. But she also recognized that danger stalked people like Minnie whenever they ventured too far from home. Everyone knew that. Elders on the reserve warned children dreaming of a better life in the city. Parents cautioned anxious teenagers about urban centres where there were few native people. Even some of those who, like Minnie, had wanted to get out of the community since they were adolescents, had realized that they were better off staying where they were wanted, where they would be safe. If Minnie had ever been remotely affected by such a trend, her actions never showed it.

When her chores were done, Christy went out for a walk. She passed a few people who knew Minnie and who probably hadn't heard the news. But she just smiled and said hello. A few houses down from hers, she left the road and made her way along a short cut to the main drag. She sneaked along the path, cleared of snow by many crossings, to avoid an encounter with some friends she spotted in the distance who would want to stop and chat. Once on the street that skirted the near-frozen Albany River, she decided to walk in the direction of the airport. Though a regular pastime among the inhabitants of Kashechewan, Christy was never one to be interested in who was arriving, or to stand on the runway and envy a planeload of departing residents. But today, she craved such novelty, if only to imagine flying off to visit her friend in one of those magical places about which she had heard. As hard as she tried, though, it didn't work. All she could conjure in her head was the sad truth that Minnie, as Christy knew her, would never fly into that airport again and the painful certainty that, this time, Minnie had really flown away for good.

Coroner's Inquest Testimony – Dr. Vitale Montpetit

Q. Any other injuries on the body anywhere? You've indicated the head. Anywhere else on the body which were not consistent with medical treatment?

A. There were two areas of the body which we didn't think that these lesions were related to medical treatment. One was–consisted of multiple healing abrasions on the medial aspect of the right forearm and the other one was an ovoid fairly large bruise in the right calf medial aspect of the right calf.

Q. O.K. If you could just describe first of all the forearm and could you just show us where you're talking about?

A. (Witness complies.)

Q. All right. Indicating the forearm, and what did you find there?

A. Multiple abrasion of the skin, healing. They weren't a couple of days. They were more like seven, ten days or...

Q. Um-hmm. And consistent with what kind of–consistent with trauma of some sort?

A. Could have been due to trauma, most likely. It couldn't–I didn't have any other explanation other than trauma, really.

Q. Is this something that you see in accident victims who may have come in contact with the pavement or roadway or...?

A. That would be a possible explanation.

No one asked me anything, or cared
about what I had to say.
— CHIEF JONATHAN SOLOMON

Minnie's death finally set in motion an investigation by the Hull police. Persistent newspaper reporters set up camp at Hull's police headquarters and asked frank and sometimes leading questions of anyone who passed by. Letter after letter from outraged citizens churned out of the station's fax machine, fuelled by the day's newspaper headlines or radio announcements. Demands for an explanation poured in by mail and courier from angry interest groups.

The Hull police were ready for the assault.

Patrick Smith had called the Hull police to report Minnie's hospitalization right after he alerted the Ottawa General Hospital about the accident. Like the hospital's social worker, he, too, had difficulty reaching someone who was either interested in or responsible for the incident he was reporting. After repeating his story to some fifteen different people, he reached Captain Armand Caron.

A day or so after the call, Captain Caron stopped by Patrick's apartment with another officer. Before the meeting, Patrick had been hopeful that, at last, the two officers might be taken to task for their actions. But both men only questioned Patrick about the perceived arrogance he and his friends had exhibited toward officers Regimbald and Vincent, and about the boys' overall state of sobriety. Well on his way to a career in social work, Patrick could see that Caron's line of questioning served little purpose, particularly when the investigation continued to focus on the actions of everyone except those who had an obligation to be responsible. He knew that to conduct a proper investigation these men would have to accept that an *accident*, not an *incident*, had occurred, that Minnie had been hit by a car, and that she ended up in a hospital, either directly or indirectly, as a result of it. But to acknowledge this would be akin to admitting that two of their officers had acted negligently.

Patrick and Michel left for Acapulco the following day, wondering what more could go wrong. When they returned the following week, Minnie's face was on the front page of every local and regional paper, and Patrick's answering machine was crammed with messages from reporters.

Police Statement – *Hull Police Accident Investigator Constable Michael Bastien*
This witness will indicate that witness Filion gave in his statement that Minnie Sutherland had been walking on the sidewalk and attempted to cross the street and had fallen from a snowbank onto the roadway and that she had picked herself up and continued to walk across the street where she was struck by the vehicle. He indicates that the motor vehicle hit Minnie Sutherland with its front and that the victim rolled off the hood of the car onto the street.

The strategy used by the Hull police to defend the two officers implicated was unwittingly handed to them by the very people who were pointing accusing fingers in their direction. First, there was the media, who rather than tackle the issue head-on were trying to prove that Minnie had not been drunk. Instead, they were trying to show that, since Minnie was diabetic, perhaps she was disoriented, in need of a shot of insulin, and that she was blind, which likely made matters worse. Consequently, the media reporting turned into a crusade against stereotyping Minnie as a drunk Indian, avoiding the crucial issue that, drunk or not, Indian or white, Minnie Sutherland was entitled to proper care.

Then there was the hospital, which had carelessly put needles into Minnie's arteries twice—the second time minutes before she died. This mistake, which was quickly corrected, had little to do with her death but still gave the Hull police the opportunity to deflect some of the criticism onto the hospital.

Finally there were two of the witnesses: Minnie's cousin, Joyce Wesley, whose story changed from interview to interview; and, perhaps most important, the nurse, Carole St-Denis, who, while outraged by the police officers' inaction, continued to insist that Minnie was not hit by her car, but, rather, had walked into it.

Police Statement – *Constable Michael Bastien*
This witness will indicate that he received information from the RCMP lab that blue paint had been found on the victim's clothing and because of this paint samples were taken from the vehicle that was owned and driven by Ms. St. Denis.

Maggie Bugden didn't recognize the woman who lay in the grey casket at the Racine, Robert and Gauthier funeral home. One of the attendants explained that they didn't have a photograph on which to rely when they were putting Minnie's head back together following the autopsy. *Oh, she wore glasses, did she?*

The memorial service had been arranged in part by the Ottawa General Hospital. As was often the case when no family members are around to manage the funeral and no money is available to pay for anything, the nurses at the General called Maurice Prud'homme, the funeral home's director, and asked if he would help out.

Prud'homme offered the use of a parlour at no cost, the loan of a casket for the day, and free embalming services. He didn't expect many people to show up for the service; no members of the immediate family lived in town and the body was being shipped up north for the funeral. Nevertheless, he arranged the room by setting up several sprays of flowers from another parlour that had been vacated, and called on Reverend Gary McCauley, a local minister who claimed to have known Minnie, to volunteer time for the service.

At first it seemed as if no one was going to come; then, one by one, a few native people, some of whom knew one another, started to arrive. Conversations were subdued, even cautious. The mourners greeted each other politely, and, in a couple of cases exchanged commentaries on the incident that had brought them together that day. "I can't believe what the police did," said one person. The standard reply: "You know what the Quebec police are like." Then, "But why didn't that nurse stay there in the first place?" Most of the natives stopped short of laying any blame on Joyce, as she was within earshot of many such conversations.

Maggie Budgen was sombre throughout the service. She sat quietly with her daughter, Cita, on one of the sofas, greeting people as if she were a member of Minnie's immediate family.

Joyce sat close by, expressing outrage to any native passerby as if she were just hearing the tragic news that instant; when a white person came near, she became tight-lipped. Doreen wheeled herself into the room and right up in front of Joyce, blocking the few reporters who had wandered in and had taken to asking any native-looking individual if Joyce Wesley was there.

Tim Milbury stood guard at the door, talking fondly of Minnie to one of the funeral home attendants, who was unaware of the controversy surrounding Minnie's death until one of the reporters poked his head into the main office and asked which room Minnie Sutherland was in and if pictures were allowed.

Evelyn Mark was there, too, keeping mostly to herself, but chatting with a younger woman who everyone assumed was her daughter. She kept telling people who greeted her that "all Minnie wanted to do was go see the fireworks and look what happened."

Several people from native groups attended, accompanied by three or four whites who looked like lawyers. Maggie recognized one of the women: Marsha Smoke from the Cree Naskapi Commission. She and the others stood quietly to one side while Reverend McCauley conducted the service, reading passages from the Bible and ending with a passionate eulogy that left even the strangers wet-eyed. When the service ended, the lawyer types whispered among themselves and gave a statement to one reporter—something about a public inquiry—then quickly departed.

Maggie Bugden stayed longer, telling Cita stories about the times she had spent with Minnie, especially the first year they had spent together in Ottawa. Then she and Cita left, too, wondering on their way out where Evelyn had disappeared to. Joyce was the last to leave, tailing Tim and Doreen, who cleared the way of any reporters who might be hanging around outside.

That afternoon, Minnie was moved out of the casket and into a shipping container for the ride to the airport and connecting flights to Toronto, Timmins, Moosonee, Fort Albany, and finally, Kashechewan.

Minnie's funeral was held in Kashechewan at the end of the second week of January 1989. Long before the service began, the pews in St. Paul's Anglican Church had started to fill and the usual row of men who stood at the back had already started to form. By the time the family arrived, the church was more than half-full, allowing any outbursts of emotion at the sight of Minnie's lifeless body to be lost in the sound of voices and shuffle of heels tapping along the wooden floor.

Before the service began, Minnie's casket lay open inside the church entrance, just behind the double doors through which the guests arrived. After the family had spent a few minutes with Minnie, they made their way to the front of the church. Then other guests filed in. The people of Kashechewan expressed their sympathy in the usual ways: a few words of condolence for the family, a kiss on the deceased person's forehead, a gentle pat on her cold hands.

As each visitor in the procession gave way to another, Roseanne stole glances toward the casket. She had a difficult time believing that the body inside—particularly the face—belonged to her mother, and reasoned that the people who had prepared her body for burial were either in a hurry or didn't have any appreciation of what her mother looked like.

She thought about how she had never really known the side of her mother that was drawn to the excitement—and the anonymity —of big cities, and about how what she did know left her feeling more like an understanding sister than a daughter. Looking at her mother, she contemplated her own life, before the arrival of her baby, when her grandparents had taken on the role normally shared by mother and father. For her mother's choices all those years, Roseanne was more grateful than bitter. For Minnie's death and the circumstances under which it occurred, she was more outraged than sad.

Once the minister gave the signal, the casket was closed and eight pallbearers carried Minnie to the front of the church. Instantly, the congregation rose and broke out in hymn. Roseanne, Violet, and their grandmother sat in the front row; Linda, John, and their children sat behind. Assisting in the service was Chief Jonathan Solomon, draped in the robe commonly worn by laypeople who participate in a church service.

Linda fought back tears for most of the service, looking over at the casket from time to time, and exchanging comforting looks with Roseanne whenever she turned around, and with Christy Wesley.

Maggie Sutherland sobbed intermittently throughout the service, taking care to control her emotions and remain dignified. Once the service was over, she followed the casket outside, holding Violet's hand tightly and declining all offers for an escort.

The pallbearers hoisted the casket into a truck for the short drive to the cemetery. On arrival, one of the men misjudged the depth of the snow and slipped, causing a couple of others to lose their footing and nearly drop the coffin. *What else can go wrong?* thought Roseanne.

Knowing from a week or so after Minnie's death that some form of inquiry was likely to be held, Roseanne, Linda, and John delayed flying to Ottawa to clean out Minnie's apartment until they had some idea of when their presence might again be required. Finally, in early February, they accompanied Chief Jonathan Solomon south to be part of the official announcement of the Coroner's Inquest into the Death of Minnie Sutherland.

Roseanne had arranged to meet her aunt Linda and Joyce Wesley at the apartment in Mechanicsville. By the time she arrived, Minnie's belongings had already been stuffed into a couple of suitcases and a few boxes. Soon after, a Salvation Army truck rolled up and collected the few pieces of furniture that Minnie had owned. The rest belonged to the landlord and would remain in the apartment for the tenant due to move in the first of March.

❦

While in Ottawa, Roseanne and Linda attended meetings with their lawyer, David Nahwegahbow, and his co-counsel, Sharon McIvor, of the Native Women's Association of Canada.

Once the inquest was publicly announced, Linda and Roseanne were faced with a deluge of requests from the media for interviews. *How do you feel about the inquest? Do you believe race was a factor in the actions of the Hull police? Do you think Minnie was thought to be drunk because she wasn't wearing her glasses and couldn't see? Are you planning to sue?*

Jonathan Solomon sat quietly at the meetings. As the symbolic head of all families on the reserve, he felt he should be there, and Minnie's family wished to accord him this respect even a thousand miles away. But for the people handling the business of the inquest, a reserve chief served no visible purpose. They had nothing to ask of him. And, as Jonathan Solomon soon realized, he had nothing to offer.

Later that spring, Minnie's purse, missing since shortly after her admission to the Ottawa General Hospital, turned up.

It was found in the unit where Carole St-Denis, the woman whose car had hit Minnie, worked. Following the death of another female patient, a family member came to collect her mother's personal belongings—in particular, a key for a safe deposit box in the hospital. While searching the closet at the nurse's station, Carole came across two purses and grabbed the closest one. When the deceased woman's daughter noticed a pack of cigarettes in the purse, she insisted that this couldn't be the right purse—her mother didn't smoke.

After the woman left with the right purse, Carole looked through the other bag. Under the cigarettes she found a pair of bifocals with dark rims, and beneath them a pair of sunglasses and an Ontario Health Card that read: SUTHERLAND, MINNIE.

AFTER

Shock governed my initial reaction to the jury's verdict. It was unfathomable to think that four of the five jurors believed that racism had nothing to do with the way Minnie Sutherland had been treated by the police, and that mere training would prevent such an incident from happening again.

I wasn't the only person who was sceptical of the verdict. Jim Eagle, director of the Odawa Native Friendship Centre, was quoted in the article as saying that "the inquest was a practice in futility," and that it "created a false sense of something being done." Sharon McIvor, the lawyer representing the Native Women's Association of Canada, rejected the jury's recommendation as "airy-fairy," stating her conviction that "the jury's finding won't have a significant impact on preventing a repeat of the Sutherland incident."

McIvor had good reason to take issue with the verdict. Refused standing at the outset of the inquest, she had been forced to settle for being co-counsel to Roseanne's lawyer, David Nahwegahbow. Then, the courtroom heard the taped call to Hull police headquarters describing Minnie as a "squaw," prompting the judge to give her full and immediate standing. From then on, McIvor interrogated witnesses with passion and determination, certain that she would prove that things would have turned out differently had Minnie been white.

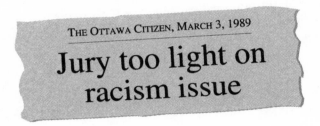

THE OTTAWA CITIZEN, MARCH 3, 1989

Jury too light on racism issue

The next day, the dissenting juror, who asked not to be identified, spoke out, insisting that "We could have brought it up, not to accuse anybody, but to show there is racism." The unnamed juror seemed to support McIvor's sentiments, which included her desire for the jury to "acknowledge racism" as a part of the tragedy, "but they categorically avoided that word."

Everyone following the case noticed the absence of a comment from Roseanne in the media reports. Apparently, she had disappeared from the hearing before the verdict was even read—something about her grandmother being gravely ill in a hospital two hours away. Those who guessed at what her reaction might be tempered upset and disappointment with the hope that the findings of the Quebec Police Commission's investigation, still to be held, would offer some resolution.

THE OTTAWA CITIZEN, SEPTEMBER 1, 1990

Hull police cleared of racism in traffic death of native woman

Two Hull police officers who left a native woman by the side of the road after she had been hit by a car were negligent in their investigation of the incident, the Quebec Police Commission has concluded.

But the long-awaited report, released Friday, says Hull constables Denis Regimbald and Guy Vincent were not racially motivated when they failed to fully investigate the accident that eventually led to the death of Minnie Sutherland.

It was summer 1993 and more than four years had passed since I had first read about the verdict in the coroner's inquest; almost three had slipped by since the Quebec Police Commission's investigation had reached its conclusion.

I no longer felt angry about the tame results of these investigations, and had lost some of my cynicism about justice for the likes of Minnie Sutherland. In the end I had come to terms with the belief that Minnie's death was as much a failure in all of us who rely on the system as it was a breakdown in the system itself. Still horrified by the notion that racism played no part in Minnie's demise, I had come to the conclusion that New Year's Eve 1988 was much more about folly than calculation, its tragic events driven more by assumption than by indifference.

But I was still curious about the person at the heart of the case and whether Minnie's soul was finally at rest. And where? In the north—her home and the territory she abandoned? Or in the city, her refuge and, in the end, a place where she had been left to her own devices?

One winter evening, as I pondered the case and its outcome, I called Roseanne in Timmins and invited myself to visit her family's home in Kashechewan the following summer. During the call, I discovered two things: that Maggie Sutherland, who I had longed to meet, had died right after the inquest into her daughter's death; and that one day, I would write about the death and life of Minnie Sutherland.

LATER

The smell of Kentucky Fried Chicken filled the air, at least at the back of the plane where I was sitting. There must have been fifty–a hundred–buckets back there. Probably for some event, I thought, like a commemoration. It smelled good, familiar.

As the pilot announced our descent into Fort Albany, named for the original Cree settlement along the river, I looked through the window and followed the ribbon of cobalt through the green. There, I spotted Kashechewan. From a thousand feet up, and twenty miles distant, it looked like an abandoned trailer park.

We stayed no more than five minutes on the runway at Fort Albany. As we lifted off, I asked someone across the aisle what the rambling white building just under the wing was. She told me that it used to be a residential school but now it was a factory. Next to it, the spire of a church reached up to us.

Before the buildings of Fort Albany were out of sight, Kashechewan was below. We landed with a thud on a dirt patch that began right at the river's edge. The plane bumped along the ground and came to a halt at a tiny cabin next to a fence scaled with rust. I looked for a sign that announced Kashechewan, but there wasn't one; people rising from their seats told me that this was home.

�

The man who met me at the airport stood inside the gate, greeting passengers as they trickled off the plane. As I passed through the gate, he rushed over to his pickup to pull open the passenger door.

"Where do you want to go first?" he asked.

As he had not yet introduced himself, I wondered if he was Kashechewan's current chief, Andrew Reuben, who had told me over the telephone that someone would meet me when I arrived. But this man's voice was not that of Chief Reuben. I got in and asked how far it was to the reserve office.

My driver said nothing the entire way. The sounds of the pass-

ing trucks and the honk of an oncoming Jeep were welcome dis-
tractions as we rode along, picking up speed at each stretch, bumping around curves and dodging potholes. We passed a shanty that
edged the road, then made a sharp turn onto the strip of packed
earth that was the main drag in Kashechewan. The inhabitants of
this place came into view; most were just hanging around talking,
or fanning away the dust and sand that each passing vehicle
churned up. Some prefabricated bungalows, lined up neatly in a
row, provided a backdrop for the shacks that otherwise dominated
the view. I spotted a video store, then another store with a big
Coca-Cola sign. The pickup slowed, and the driver pointed to a
small two-storey wood-frame building that sat next to a store
labelled *NORTHERN*. As he pulled into the dusty parking lot that
hosted more people than vehicles, I decided that I had better say
something. But my driver beat me to it. He told me that he was
Minnie's brother-in-law, John Wynne, and that his wife, Linda,
would be at work all day; I could come over later.

As I stepped from the pickup, I noticed buckets of Kentucky
Fried Chicken being unloaded in front of the store. I asked John if
I could bring some over for dinner, not knowing at the time that it
would cost fifty dollars for a bucket and that I would need two to
feed everyone that would be there.

�

Everyone included Linda and John's four children and Minnie's
daughter, Violet.

The children giggled and ran in and out of the living room
while I asked Linda questions that, for the most part, John
answered. When I asked Linda how she had felt when she heard
that a book about Minnie was being written, she turned from me
and stared out the window. Seconds later, her barely audible
response came: "That someone cared."

I made an effort to curb the sombre mood caused by my question by telling Linda about stopping in Timmins on the way up to

visit Roseanne. Linda asked how her niece's lawsuit against the Hull police was going. Started shortly after the Quebec Police Commission cleared its officers of racism charges in 1990, the lawsuit was at a standstill, each step forward thwarted by clever resistance by the City of Hull's lawyers. For both Linda and me, talk of the inquiry evoked disturbing memories, as when Marcel Beaudry, a lawyer representing the two Hull police officers, entered the courtroom and greeted colleagues by saying "How." The thoughtless racial stereotype underpinning this comment may have brought laughter to the courtroom that day, but all it did now was make Linda turn away in silence.

I quickly realized that my attempt to have a pleasant conversation with Linda was failing miserably. So I repeated a conversation that Roseanne and I had shared, about how much Minnie enjoyed fireworks, and about how much she would have enjoyed the display that New Year's Eve. Especially if it had been combined with an admiring glance in the dark from some man she fancied. Then Minnie would have wrapped her arms around herself in the usual way and declared, "It's a sign of the year to come."

After dinner, John escorted me to the video store run by Minnie and Linda's brother, Sidney. He was pleasant, but talked about Minnie as if she were a stranger.

"Yeah, it was bad," he agreed, then jerked his head forward a couple of times. "But what can you do?"

On Linda's urging, John took me to meet Christy Wesley and her husband, David. Christy said little; she appeared apprehensive talking to a stranger—especially a white one—and though she could speak English, answered most of my questions by whispering to her husband in Cree. David translated more than one time how much Minnie used to make Christy laugh.

David Wesley listened to me describe my unsuccessful efforts to meet his sister, Joyce. The day after I had first spoken to Roseanne about my plans to write a book, I made my first attempt to persuade Joyce to share with me some of her thoughts about what had happened that night. I promised not to judge her actions. I said I would leave my tape recorder at home. Joyce's sister, Doreen, even pitched in to help, telling Joyce that I wasn't out to cause her harm, or to blame her for anything. "He's nice," Doreen had reassured her. Still, the closest I came to an interview was hearing Joyce's clear voice over the telephone tell me, "No, I don't want to talk about it."

The next thing I knew, David was on the phone, listening to Joyce tell him *no* as well. I thanked him for his efforts. Then, just as John and I were about to leave, the phone rang.

"It's Joyce," David said, and passed the phone to me.

Joyce said she had known I was in town before David called. I asked her how, to which she replied that news travel fast in Kash. She also said that she had seen me with John Wynne at the Northern store, when she was picking up her bucket of chicken.

Joyce asked me to understand her reluctance in discussing Minnie and all that had happened that New Year's Eve. When I asked if I could meet with her, briefly, she said "Come over in an hour."

Before dropping me off at Joyce's house, John Wynne suggested that while I was in Kash I should take the time to meet Dorothy Friday, one of Kashechewan's elders. He said I could walk there from Joyce's house.

ℰ∂

Joyce said little during my forty-five minutes with her. She shared some insights, mostly about how she distrusted the authorities, especially after she witnessed how the Hull police had treated Minnie that New Year's Eve. She seemed convinced that people lied during the inquest and that her state of sobriety that night had made her the obvious scapegoat. I didn't have to ask if she felt responsible in any way for Minnie's death: she had already implied in many ways that she did.

ℰ∂

Dorothy Friday owned the house just down the road from Christy and David Wesley. A tipi used for treating moose hides, which Dorothy cut and made into moccasins, stood in her backyard.

Dorothy recalled on my behalf a not-so-distant past when she spent a great deal of her time taking children into the bush, teaching them how to use the land to heal themselves if they were sick or injured. Lately, she spent more time minding her five-year-old granddaughter while her son and daughter-in-law worked at nine-to-five jobs on the reserve.

She obligingly showed me her tipi, which was draped with blue and orange plastic tarps, and gave me a quick lesson in stretching animal skins. Behind us, her young granddaughter teased me with smiles and tricks, giggling every time her antics captured my attention. I was invited in for a drink. I expected to see a bucket of chicken sitting on the counter but there wasn't one.

Dorothy didn't know Minnie well, but was saddened by her fate. Yes, she knew where Minnie was buried and that no headstone marked her grave, but she wasn't concerned about Minnie's soul. She didn't blame anyone for what had happened. Did she think it was possible for natives and whites to live in harmony? She just smiled and waited for my next question.

I left after a short while, just before the sun fell behind the trees on the far side of the river. Dorothy waved goodbye, then watched her granddaughter follow me down the road, first on tricycle, then on foot.

I passed a couple of houses, then turned around. The little girl tittered and shuffled backwards, at once excited and shy. When I continued walking, she started after me.

Another house slipped by before I looked back again to find the little girl treading cautiously behind. This time when I started up, though, she didn't follow. Instead, she stopped in her tracks, looked over her shoulder to the reassuring figure of her grandmother, then turned to face me again. I noticed that the smile so radiant moments before was gone; no laugh bubbled up.

She started to run, not toward me this time, but back toward her grandmother. As she ran, she picked up the pace. Faster. Faster. Now, I was the one to stop, but unlike the little girl, not to change my direction. Just to watch a child run back to her grandmother, her tipi, and tales about spirits on the other side of the sun, healers in the woods, and the dreams that walk beside you.

Flores, José, 86-87
Four Corners (Hull), 59, 65, 76,
    79, 86
Four Jays (restaurant), 98, 99,
    112
Friday, Dorothy, 190, 191
Froh, James, 136

G Givogue, Luc, 111-13
    police statement of, 112
    testimony of, 112-13
Goodwin, Barbara, 27
Goodwin, Thomas, 27

H Halgerson, Sherry, 38
Hamon, François, 17
Harris, Walter, 16
Hébert, Paul, 143
Hill, Mary, 129, 132
Hudon, Carl, 105, 106-7, 108
Hull (Quebec):
    bars in. *See* Strip, the
    911 service to, 88
    and Ottawa, link with,
        57-58, 59
Hull Bar Association, 17
Hull police, 14, 15, 16
    conduct of, in treatment of Minnie,
        13, 14, 15, 79-83, 88-89, 156, 162, 163, 171
    internal investigation, 16, 17
    lawsuit against, 189
    medical report to, 15, 161-63
    QPC ruling concerning, 183, 189
    taped call to, 84, 182

I Ibrahim, Abdi, 90-94, 95, 96-102
    testimony of, 91, 96
Inquiries. *See* Coroner's Inquest into the
    Death of Minnie Sutherland; Public
    inquiries; Quebec Police Commission
Irving, Karen, 85

J

Jonah, Beatrice, 121, 132
Jones, Gwynne, 15
  report to Hull police, 15, 161-63
  testimony of, 143, 158
J. R. Dallas (bar), 54, 59, 66, 75,
  77, 83, 96, 144, 154

K

Kashechewan, 17, 28, 29, 30,
  64, 133, 135, 138, 139, 149-53,
  175-77, 184, 187-92
Khan, Gabriel, 143, 144
Kicknosway, Vince, 35
Knox, David, 15, 57, 65, 77, 82, 83,
  84, 85, 87-90, 93

L

Lebreton Flats, 95
Le Pub, 65-66, 77
Letters:
  Gwynne Jones to Hull police,
    15, 161-63
  Minnie to Daisy Arthur, 35-37

M

McCauley, Gary, 174, 175
McIvor, Sharon, 17, 177, 181-82
Madore, Kelly, 48, 51, 52, 53
Maple Leaf (bar), 124
Mark, Evelyn, 31, 33, 34, 40-41,
  43-44, 47, 48, 49, 53, 61, 67, 68, 121,
  135, 136, 137-38, 141, 154, 174-75
Martel, Yves, 14
Mechanicsville, 23-25, 34-35, 95, 97
Mexi-Go, 86-91
Milbury, Doreen, 23, 26, 34, 139, 141,
  142, 153, 155, 159, 165, 174, 175, 190
Milbury, Tim, 26, 34, 139, 142, 153, 155,
  159, 174, 175
  testimony of, 34
Moloughney, Brian, 101-2
  testimony of, 101, 102, 103
Montpetit, Vitale, testimony of,
  164-65, 167, 169
Moose Factory, 28, 34, 120, 132, 142